Using
UNIX®

Phillip Laplante
Fairleigh Dickinson University

Robert Martin

West Publishing Company
Minneapolis/St. Paul • New York • Los Angeles • San Francisco

Trademarks

All products are trademarks or registered trademarks of their respective holders.

About the Authors

Phil Laplante, assistant professor of computer science at Fairleigh Dickinson University, holds a PhD in computer science and a professional engineering license in the state of New Jersey. He has extensive experience programming in the C language using the Unix operating system for various Fortune 100 companies. He has published numerous papers and two other books.

Rob Martin is a systems analyst and software engineer working in the telecommunications industry. He has six years of experience designing and developing systems for various Unix platforms.

Dedication

To our wives, Nancy and Cj, for their support and encouragement during the many hours devoted to this project, and to Dr. Peter Falley for his inspiration.

WEST'S COMMITMENT TO THE ENVIRONMENT

In 1906, West Publishing Company began recycling materials left over from the production of books. This began a tradition of efficient and responsible use of resources. Today, up to 95% of our legal books and 70% of our college and school texts are printed on recycled, acid-free stock. West also recycles nearly 22 million pounds of scrap paper annually—the equivalent of 181,717 trees. Since the 1960s, West has devised ways to capture and recycle waste inks, solvents, oils, and vapors created in the printing process. We also recycle plastics of all kinds, wood, glass, corrugated cardboard, and batteries, and have eliminated the use of Styrofoam book packaging. We at West are proud of the longevity and the scope of commitment to the environment.

Production, Prepress, Printing and Binding by West Publishing Company.

Contents

iv

List of Figures

List of Tables

Background and Objectives

This book is an introduction to the Unix operating system for programmers. In particular, its purpose is to assist programmers who are students of the C language and find themselves confronted with Unix. It is intended to supplement a typical C programming text used in C language courses. This book may also be used by those who are learning to program in C on the Unix operating system without the benefit of an instructor, or as an introduction for non-programmers.

Many introductory C language courses use a version of Unix as the operating system of choice. This is natural since Unix and C co-evolved and co-exist in many industrial and academic settings. Furthermore, the Unix operating system offers a rich programming environment on processing systems ranging from desktop personal computers to the most powerful supercomputers.

While there are many excellent texts on Unix, some of which are mentioned in the bibliography, many of these are too detailed for an introductory C course and the novice user. This text is designed specifically for novices.

Organization and Flexibility

Our primary goal is to provide a sufficient introduction to the Unix operating system so that the student can prepare, compile, and run C programs quickly and efficiently.

Chapter 1 describes fundamental Unix concepts. In particular, the file system, Unix processes, and the command processor are described in detail. In addition, user accounts, the system administrator, and certain security aspects are introduced. Chapter 1 is the foundation for the rest of the text.

Chapter 2 describes how to log on and off a Unix system and how to maintain a password, and it also presents essential Unix commands. Shell variables, the environment, and file name generation are described in detail. In addition, this chapter describes some of the Unix shell's advanced features, such as input/output re-direction and pipelines. It also contains an introduction to advanced commands.

Chapter 3 is a self-contained guide to the visual text editor **vi**. It describes text file structure and the **vi** commands used to create, modify, and maintain text files—notably C source code files. Regular expressions, copying and moving text, and other editing techniques are included.

Chapter 4 discusses compilation and debugging commands and their use in preparing, running, and debugging C language programs. In particular, the use of the compiler, assembler, and linker is described. Useful utilities, such as **lint** and **cb**, are also covered. A discussion of source code control and application maintenance tools is included at an introductory level.

Other audiences will also find this text useful. This includes ordinary users, individuals programming in a language other than C, and students of another topic related to Unix. These readers may consider one of the following alternatives:

- Readers who want immediate hands-on information may focus on Chapters 2 and 3, using Chapter 1 as a reference.

- Readers who are not interested in advanced topics may omit the final two sections of Chapter 2.

- Readers who prefer an editor other than **vi** may skip Chapter 3.

- Readers not interested in C programs may concentrate on Chapters 1, 2, and 3, skipping Chapter 4.

Finally, we hope that this text provides enough material to motivate the student to further study of the Unix operating system. The bibliography is a source of additional information on Unix.

Features

This book introduces the reader to Unix from the perspective of a programmer. While other books assume the reader wishes to learn Unix for its own sake, we recognize that many students wish to learn Unix to create and run programs. The book has the following additional features:

- The material is presented clearly and concisely.

- The text is suitable for both the classroom and self-study.

- Each chapter is self-contained.

- The text makes extensive use of graphic illustrations and examples.

- Appendices supplement the text and make it more compact.

- An extensive glossary and index are provided.

- Exercises are provided in each chapter to challenge readers and enhance their understanding.

- A solutions manual is available.

Pedagogy

To keep the text compact and focused, we assume the reader is computer literate—familiar with basic computer concepts including operating systems, programming languages, compilers, and editors. This book may be a useful part of an introduction to such topics but it is not intended to be a stand-alone introduction to computers, programming, or operating systems.

Each chapter includes exercises that encourage practice and stimulate the student's understanding of Unix. In particular, certain exercises explore concepts and details that are not fully described in the text. In many cases, the reader will be led to discover and explore new aspects of Unix. Furthermore, extensive use of diagrams and figures makes the concepts easy to understand.

The examples presented in the text were developed and run on Unix System V release 4 (SVR4). This version of the operating system was selected because it contains commands and features found in other popular variants, it is widely available, and, frankly, the authors are most familiar with it. Although the examples were tested on various systems, they may produce slightly different results on the reader's system. We elected to concentrate on a single version of Unix to prevent confusion for the reader and keep the text consistent with its objectives. The concepts presented are generally applicable to other versions of Unix.

The text editor, **vi**, was selected because it is distributed with Unix SVR4. It is also widely available on other versions of Unix, and the commands are consistent across versions. Another popular editor, **emacs**, has at least four different variants. Each variant is sufficiently different so that a single coherent treatment is very difficult. A thorough introduction to **emacs** is beyond the scope of this text.

The following conventions apply throughout the text:

- Key terms appear in *this type face* when introduced.

- Example interactions with Unix appear in `this type face`.

- Unix commands appear in **this type face**.

- Control keys appear as `<CTRL-d>` or `^c`.

- The carriage return is depicted as `<CR>`.

- The escape key is depicted as `<ESC>`.

4

Acknowledgements

The authors gratefully acknowledge the following friends and colleagues for their support and graciously reviewing portions of the manuscript at various draft stages for technical accuracy, completeness, and clarity:

- Sharon Adams of West Educational Publishing
- Gary Birkmaier of the Perkin Elmer Corporation
- Eugene Braun of AT&T Information Systems
- Mitch Germansky
- Peter Gordon of West Educational Publishing
- Caroline Hicks
- Lucy Paine Kezar of West Educational Publishing
- C. J. Martin
- Rick Ramirez
- Therese Saulnier

Any remaining errors and inaccuracies are the responsibility of the authors.

Chapter 1

Fundamental Unix Concepts

This chapter introduces the Unix operating system and describes some of its important characteristics. Emphasis is placed on the concepts that are essential to the new user and set an appropriate foundation for the detailed discussions, examples, and exercises that follow.

1.1   Introduction to Unix

UNIX, a registered trademark of AT&T's UNIX System Laboratories, is the common name for a family of interactive, multiuser operating systems[1]. Unix is available in one version or another for virtually any computer, ranging from desktop personal computers and workstations to the most powerful supercomputers.

Unix was originally developed on a Digital Equipment Corporation (DEC) PDP-7 in 1969 by Ken Thompson and Dennis Ritchie—employees of AT&T's Bell Laboratories. Their objective was to create a flexible, interactive processing environment suitable for programming and computer systems research projects. Unix was ported to the DEC PDP-11 during 1970–71, and by the latter half of 1971 it was busy supporting its first real world application—a text processing and typesetting system used by Bell Labs' patent department. Unix turned out to be a success at something other than arcane computer research.

Initial work on the programming language that would become C started in 1971, and the operating system kernel was rewritten in C during 1973. Prior to that time Unix was written entirely in assembly language. The popularity and application of Unix increased so much that an internal systems group was formed to support the growing number of Unix installations within Bell Labs, other AT&T departments, and the local Bell operating companies. Although at the time, AT&T was prohibited from marketing computer products, Unix was distributed without support to a number of universities for educational purposes. It was also licensed to commercial institutions during the 1970s. During the late 1970s and early 1980s several versions of Unix internal to AT&T were combined to create Unix System III. System V, which evolved out of System III, was released commercially and officially supported in 1983. At the time, the number of Unix installations was approaching 100,000 worldwide.

Unix System V has seen several upgrades, feature additions, and a continued rise in popularity since its initial release. Several other versions of Unix, rooted in the educational and commercial releases of the 1970s, have also taken hold in the marketplace. The popularity of Unix is attributed,

---

[1]UNIX is not an acronym, and therefore need not be capitalized unless referring to the registered trademark. Throughout the text we use the term Unix.

in part, to a growing number of systems professionals who were educated in a Unix environment. It is also attributed, in part, to its portability. About 95 percent of Unix is written in the C programming language—assembly language is only used for hardware-dependent routines or to maximize performance. This makes Unix easier to port than many other operating systems. In addition, vendors are motivated to port Unix because it provides a rich and consistent environment for applications software development on a variety of different hardware platforms.

Unix is a capable multitasking system ideally suited for both stand-alone and distributed processing configurations. It has powerful yet easy-to-use hardware interface mechanisms and provides an excellent means of organizing and storing files on a variety of media including magnetic disks, magnetic tapes, and optical disks. Unix systems are available to support individual users, small groups, or entire departments on a wide range of processing platforms.

1.2 The Unix Family

System V is the Unix version officially supported by AT&T's UNIX System Laboratories (USL). System V is distributed by AT&T for both microcomputers and minicomputers. Other licensed vendors distribute System V for everything from desktop machines to supercomputers. USL also produces the System V Interface Definition (SVID), which determines how well any version of Unix complies with System V standards. Depending on the software manufacturer and the hardware platform, different versions of System V may vary. However, if a given Unix implementation complies with the SVID, it is more receptive to applications developed on different platforms.

Berkeley Software Distribution (BSD) was developed at the University of California at Berkeley and originally released in 1977. BSD evolved from the Unix Time-Sharing System Sixth Edition—a predecessor of System III. BSD was one of the first versions of Unix to provide demand paging, virtual memory, and support for high-speed local area networks. In 1980, BSD 4.0 became the standard Unix platform for the Defense Advanced Research Projects Agency (DARPA) network development and the latest release, BSD 4.3, includes support for ISO/OSI networks. BSD is widely used on minicomputers.

XENIX is a version of Unix produced and distributed explicitly for personal computers (PCs). Originally developed by Microsoft and released in 1986, XENIX is currently distributed by Santa Cruz Operation (SCO) and Interactive for computers based on Intel's 80X86 line of microprocessors. Since XENIX was designed for PCs, it is smaller and generally provides better performance than PC versions of System V. However, the performance gap between XENIX and System V (for PCs) will close as faster and more capable microprocessors, such as Intel's 80486 and 80586, reach the marketplace.

One of AT&T's objectives for System V was to set a standard for all versions of Unix to follow. A controversy and something of a struggle within the Unix community ensued following the release of System V. As of this writing, several competing standards exist or are under development. Each of the major players in the Unix marketplace believe their version offers something unique—something that should be preserved. AT&T has since modified its strategy. In conjunction with AT&T, Sun Microsystems developed SunOS, a version of Unix for its workstations and file servers, which combines features from both System V and BSD. The latest AT&T release, System V Release 4 (SVR4), incorporates important features from SunOS, BSD, and XENIX. SVR4 also includes a C compiler that conforms to the ANSI X3J11 international standard.

Other operating systems exhibit features that are based on or similar to those of Unix. MINIX is a microcomputer operating system produced for the purpose of educating students about the design and development of operating systems. The features of MINIX are compatible with those of System VII, one of System V's predecessors. MINIX is available with source code and a supporting textbook. Microsoft's Disk Operating System (MS-DOS), the popular personal computer operating system, also has many features that are similar to those of Unix.

1.3 What is an Operating System?

An operating system is a complex program (or series of programs) that makes a computer both useful and practical. An operating system such as Unix is responsible for the following:

- providing device drivers and interface services that allow access to the computer's hardware

- providing interrupt handlers and device service routines to support the hardware itself

- scheduling tasks for execution by the central processing unit (CPU)

- arbitrating and resolving contention for hardware and system services

- managing memory and magnetic disk space

• processing user's commands

From a user's perspective, an operating system is the means of running applications programs and accessing the computer's resources. It is one of the user's most important tools. A user's primary concern is applications—spreadsheets, word processors, and the like—and the operating system is the means by which a user activates these programs. In turn, application programs access the computer's hardware via the operating system. The operating system also defines the structure and presentation of the computer's secondary storage and peripheral devices.

Admittedly, this is a simplified perspective. However, the primary interest of a novice user is to issue commands and run programs, organize the computer's disk space, and access the computer's peripherals. Therefore, it is a natural perspective for an introduction to Unix. The remainder of this chapter is devoted to these fundamental concepts. More complex considerations are better left to courses and texts offering an advanced study of Unix and systems programming. Section 1.4 describes the Unix file system—the Unix representation of disk/tape storage space and hardware devices. Understanding the file system is perhaps the most important objective for new users, so the bulk of this chapter is devoted to this topic. Section 1.5 introduces the Unix process—the Unix model of a running program. Section 1.6 provides a look at the shell—the Unix command processor. The remainder of the chapter deals with environmental issues related to Unix. Section 1.7 discusses user accounts. Section 1.8 introduces the Unix system administrator and his or her role in a Unix environment. Section 1.9 discusses some security aspects of Unix.

1.4 The Unix File System

The Unix *file system* is the means of storing and organizing programs and data as well as the interface to the computer's hardware devices. A file system contains three types of file—*ordinary files*, *special files*, and *directories*. Ordinary files include text files, data files, and programs. Special files are points of interface to the computer's hardware. Directories provide the associations between files contained by a file system and the names by which those files are known.

Figure 1.1 is a stylized representation of a Unix file system. Unix file systems are hierarchical in structure, similar to a corporate organization chart or family tree. Appearing at the top of the file system is the *root directory*—in this example the root directory is named `rootdir`. The root directory is the structural foundation for a file system. All other directories and files are built upon the root directory. In this example, the root directory contains references to ordinary files, file1 and file2, as well as references to other directories, dir1 and dir2. Similarly, dir1 and dir2 contain references to other files and other directories. Any file depicted in this example could be a special file; a directory may contain references to special files as well as to ordinary files and other directories. The hierarchical nature of a Unix file system is a consequence of the fact that directories may contain references to other directories. Therefore, directories also dictate the basic structure of a Unix file system in addition to associating files with file names.

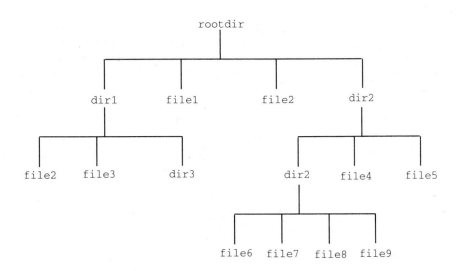

Figure 1.1: A stylized file system

Creating a Unix file system is analogous to formatting and partitioning disks and tapes in other operating systems. File systems are constructed on all types of media—magnetic disks, optical disks, and magnetic tapes. By far the most commonly used storage media is magnetic disk—Unix is essentially a disk operating system. A single disk may contain more than one distinct file system. Each such file system is similar in structure but occupies a dedicated region of the disk. A typical Unix installation consists of several interconnected file systems that span several disks. The layout of the various file systems is based upon the installation's needs. The software used in an installation, the number of users and devices it supports, and the means of backing up programs and data all factor into the number, size, and layout of an installation's component file systems.

A tape-based file system is generally used to backup a disk, to transfer a file system between two disks, or to recover a crashed system. Optical file systems are used to store large volumes of read only data or for software distribution.

The following sections describe the three file types in additional detail and also discuss file names, pathnames, the directory hierarchy, and the file system's access protection scheme.

1.4.1 Ordinary Files

An ordinary file is a randomly addressable sequence of bytes. Most files, including text files, source code, programs, and so on, are ordinary files. Unlike other operating systems, Unix does not impose a structure on or make assumptions about ordinary files. Instead, the users of an ordinary file and the programs that operate on it determine its structure. Unix treats all ordinary files in a uniform manner regardless of their content.

The following two examples describe two common ordinary files—*text files* and *binary executable files*. These files have specific yet very different structures.

Example 1.1 *A text file is a sequence of ASCII characters. Spaces, tabs, punctuation marks, and other non-alphanumeric characters delimit words. Newline characters separate lines.*

Example 1.2 *A binary executable file is a complex program file containing a* header, *a* data segment, *and a* text segment. *The header describes the file so the loader can properly transfer it to memory. The data segment contains various types of data, including ASCII strings, binary integers, binary floating point numbers, and pointers. The text segment contains the machine instructions that will be executed by the CPU when the program is run. The format and content of a binary executable file are somewhat hardware-dependent since machine instructions and data formats are defined by the underlying hardware, most notably the CPU.*

In both of these examples, the programs that use or operate on a file determine its structure. Text editors, filters, and formatters collectively define the structure of text files. Similarly, compilers, assemblers, linkers, and loaders define the structure of binary executable files. The structure of an ordinary file is unknown to the operating system. Moreover, it is unimportant. Users and programmers are free to choose a file structure that best serves their needs.

Ordinary files range in size from zero bytes up to a Unix implementation limit of well over a gigabyte (depending on the system's data block size). In practice, Unix installations constrain the size of ordinary files by limiting the number of data blocks that may be allocated to a single file. A one megabyte limit is common in many installations.

1.4.2   Directories

A directory entry consists of a name and a reference (or pointer) to a file. As discussed previously, a directory entry may refer to an ordinary file, a special file, or another directory. Directory entries are also called *links*— they link a file with its name or names. Each file name within a directory is unique. However, a file name need not be unique across a file system—a single name may appear in any number of separate directories.

In general, directory entries provide direct access to a file. The pointer refers to a system table, called an *inode*,[2] that contains a file's disk layout. A link (directory entry) that refers to an inode is called a *hard link*. Figure 1.2 depicts a hard link. The hard link points to the file's inode, which in turn gives the file's disk layout. Alternatively, a link may provide indirect access to a file by referring to another directory entry instead of an inode. A link that refers to another directory entry is called a *soft link* or *symbolic link*. Figure 1.2 also depicts a soft link.

A file may be known by more than one name. Multiple hard links may be mapped to a file's inode and more than one soft link may refer to any particular directory entry. This allows a file to have more than one direct and more than one indirect access point. However, there are constraints on direct access. A hard link is mapped only to an inode that resides in the same file system as the directory containing the link. A hard link cannot point to an inode in another file system even if the two file systems are interconnected. Soft links are not similarly constrained. They may refer to any directory entry, including another soft link, on any file system.

Sections 2.3.2 and 2.7.1 demonstrate the command used to examine a directory's content. Section 2.10.5 describes how to create links.

Unix insures that each hard link points to a valid file by counting the links that refer to a particular inode. An inode's *link count* is incremented each time a directory entry is mapped to it and decremented each time one of these entries is removed. The file itself remains intact until the last

---

[2]The term *inode*, pronounced "eye-node," is a contraction of the words index node.

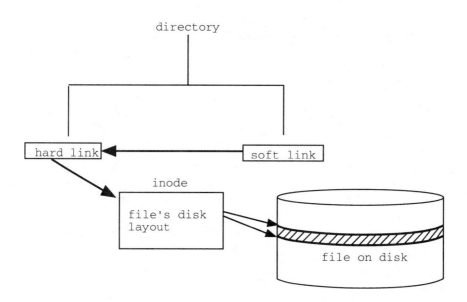

Figure 1.2: Directory entries: hard and soft links

link is removed. When the last link is removed, the link count reaches zero and Unix releases the inode and all disk space allocated to the file. In contrast, a soft link can become corrupted if its referenced directory entry is removed—Unix cannot detect this kind of error and thus cannot prevent it from occurring.

Each directory, except the root directory, has a single *predecessor* or *parent directory* and may have several *successors* or *child directories*. The root directory may have children but by definition cannot have a parent. A child directory is frequently called a *sub-directory*. The arrangement between parent and child directories guarantees the file system's integrity and gives it the hierarchical structure depicted in Figure 1.1. Figure 1.3 illustrates valid parent/child relationships between directories. The root directory, called `dira` in this example, has no parent and is the parent of `dirb` and `dirc`. The directory `dirb` has no children—`dirc` has two children, `dird` and `dire`. `dirc` is at once a parent directory and a child directory— `dira` is only a parent, and `dirb` is only a child.

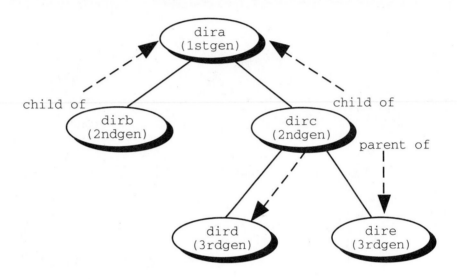

Figure 1.3: Parent/child relationships between directories

Due to its unique position in the hierarchy, the root directory is the ancestor of all other directories. Any given directory on the system, and consequently any file, can be referenced by listing in appropriate sequence the directories that descend from the root to the given directory. Conversely, ascending through the hierarchy from any directory ultimately leads to the root directory.

A system's *directory hierarchy* is usually depicted as an upside down tree. Figure 1.4 illustrates a small Unix directory hierarchy consisting of 10 directories. The root directory, named with a slash character (/), appears at the top of the hierarchy. Extending downward from the root are its children, in this example bin, home, etc, and usr, and its other descendants pal, robm, bin, include, and sys. Note that the directory name bin appears twice—once as a child of the root directory and once as a child of usr, a grandchild of the root directory. This illustrates the point that a single name may appear in several directories. Finally, the number of generations that descend from a directory is not restricted. It is common to see directory hierarchies of six or more generations.

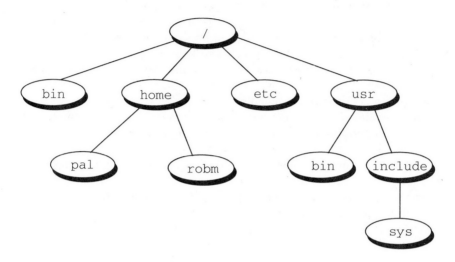

Figure 1.4: A typical directory hierarchy

1.4.3   Special Files

A *special file* is a point of interface to one of the computer's hardware devices or a synchronized communications channel between two or more cooperating programs.

The computer's random access memory, disk drives, tape drives, I/O ports, and so forth, are accessed via special files. Every such device has at least one special file associated with it. However, as the following two examples illustrate, a device may have more than one special file.

Example 1.3 *Disk drives support both character and block I/O. Each I/O mode requires a different driver. Therefore, a disk typically has one special file used for block I/O and a separate special file used for character I/O.*

Example 1.4 *Tape drives operate at different speeds both with and without tape rewind. It is common to see multiple special files defined for tape drives — one for each operational mode. Users select the operational mode they need by referring to the appropriate special file.*

A device that provides several I/O or operational modes typically has a special file associated with each such mode.

Unix provides a distinct command to create special files. However, the basic interface mechanisms (the read/write system calls) used for special files are the same ones used for ordinary files. Although device I/O involves some special considerations, command and programming syntax are generally consistent whether working with a data file or an interface to a hardware device. The intricate details of hardware devices are hidden from the user and programmer by special files. It is the operating system's responsibility to discriminate between special and ordinary files and behave appropriately. Unix recognizes I/O requests for special files and invokes the appropriate device driver to handle them.

Special files also provide a means of synchronizing and communicating between cooperating programs. A *pipe* is a one-way, first in/first out data channel between two or more programs. As illustrated in Figure 1.5, one or more programs write their output to a pipe while a separate program reads input from it. Data is received in the same order as it was written. However, the operating system does not identify or separate the output of multiple programs. Data flowing through a pipe is treated simply as a stream of bytes and the programs using it are responsible for correctly handling that data stream.

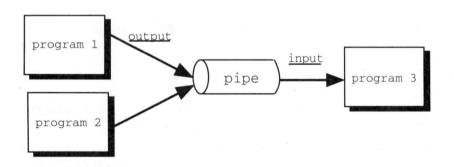

Figure 1.5: A pipe provides one-way data flow between programs

Unix synchronizes programs that share a pipe by requiring simultaneous access on each end. A program that opens a pipe for output is suspended until a program opens the same pipe for input. Conversely, a program that opens a pipe for input is blocked until at least one program opens the pipe for output.

The most common type of pipe is an *unnamed pipe*. An unnamed pipe is essentially a file without a directory entry. Unnamed pipes are temporary and persist only for the life of their client programs. There are no direct or indirect access points to an unnamed pipe. Since there are no directory entries, only the programs using an unnamed pipe have access to it.

A *named pipe* differs from an unnamed pipe in that it has at least one directory entry. Named pipes are more like ordinary files. They are generally accessible and persist until explicitly removed.

1.4.4   File and Path Names

The latest release of System V, SVR4, allows *file names* of as many as 256 characters. Prior to SVR4, Unix file names were limited to 14 characters. As illustrated by the following example, Unix is case sensitive—upper- and lowercase are distinct.

Example 1.5 *file, File and FILE are all unique names.*

Characters other than alphanumerics are permitted within file names. However, the semi-colon (;), ampersand (&), left parenthesis ((), right parenthesis ()), pipe (|), caret (^), greater-than sign (>), less-than sign (<), and minus sign (-) characters have special meaning to the command processor. These characters are frequently called *meta-characters*. The use of meta-characters file names is legal but difficult and should be avoided. It is common practice to name files using only alphanumeric characters, the underscore (_), and the period (.).

Files are referred to by *pathnames*. A pathname consists of at least a file name optionally preceded by a list of directory names. A pathname may refer to an ordinary file, a special file, or a directory since the same naming conventions apply to all file types. That is, the file name that terminates a pathname may be that of an ordinary file, a special file, or a directory.

A pathname consisting only of a file name refers to a file in the current directory. A pathname that includes a list of directories can refer to a file anywhere in the hierarchy. Directory names within a pathname are separated by slash characters (/). For this reason, slashes are not permitted within a file name except for the root directory—the root directory is referred to by a slash alone. A pathname's list of directories specifies, in appropriate order, those directories that must be traversed to locate the named file. A pathname that starts with a slash is called a *full path*. The leading slash refers to the root directory. The directory name following the leading slash refers to one of the root's children. In turn, it is followed by the name of one of the root directory's grandchildren, and so forth. A full path always refers to the same file since it uses the root directory as a reference point. Figure 1.6 illustrates the full pathnames for a portion of the example hierarchy depicted in Figure 1.4.

A *relative path* starts with something other than a slash. The first directory in the list is a child of the current directory, the second a grandchild of the current directory, and so forth. A given relative path can refer to different files since it depends on the current directory as a reference point. In Figure 1.6, the pathname `bin` can refer to `/bin` if the current directory is the root directory, or to `/usr/bin` if the current directory is `/usr`. Also, if the root is the current directory, `bin` refers to `/bin` and `usr/bin` refers to `/usr/bin`.

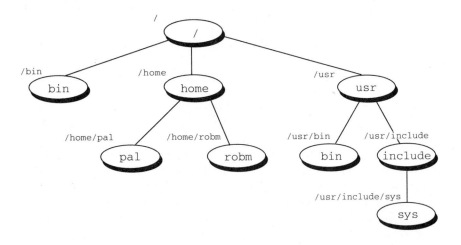

Figure 1.6: A directory hierarchy with full pathnames

Two special-purpose file names, *dot* (.) and *dot-dot* (..), appear in every directory. The file name dot refers to the directory that contains it and dot-dot refers to the parent of the directory that contains it. In other words, every directory contains a reference to itself—dot— and a reference to its parent—dot-dot. In the root directory, dot and dot-dot are equivalent since the root has no parent. These file names, illustrated in Figure 1.7, provide a means of referring to the current directory or to its parent without specifying, or even knowing, the appropriate full pathname. Furthermore, dot-dot is essential to the structure of the file system since it provides the means for ascending from a directory to its parent.

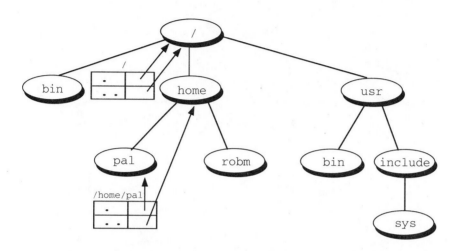

Figure 1.7: Special-purpose file names dot (.) and dot-dot (..)

1.4.5 The Directory Hierarchy

The *directory hierarchy* consists of all directories that descend from a Unix system's root directory. It may be constructed from a single file system, but more a directory hierarchy is constructed from several distinct file systems.

In a hierarchy constructed from multiple file systems, one of the file systems serves as the foundation, or root, of the hierarchy. It contains the system boot program, the root directory, and the executable *unix* program. The other file systems that comprise the hierarchy are attached to the root file system. Attaching one file system to another is analogous to splicing a branch onto a tree. A directory in the receiving file system (the tree) is replaced with the root directory of another file system (the branch).

The file systems that make up a directory hierarchy may reside on a single disk or span multiple disks. Moreover, Unix allows a file system on one host machine to be attached to the root file system of a separate computer via a local area network. These are called *remote* or *distributed* file systems. In general, the makeup of the directory hierarchy is transparent to the system's users. The same pathname conventions apply whether the hierarchy consists of a single file system, multiple file systems from multiple disks attached to a single host, or multiple file systems from multiple hosts. Regardless of a file's physical location, users can refer to and access

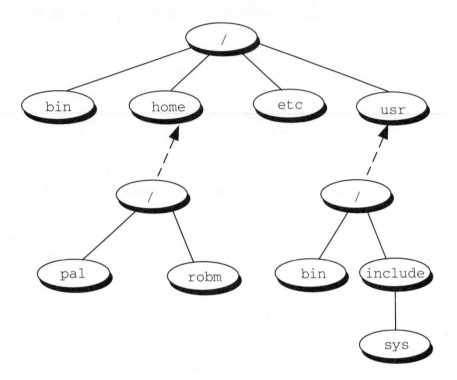

Figure 1.8: Constructing a hierarchy from multiple file systems

any file on the system (subject to access permissions explained in Section
1.4.6) without references to specific disk drives or host computers. However, certain operations, such as moving a directory, are permitted within
a single file system but not permitted between file systems even if they are
interconnected.

Figure 1.8 depicts one possible means of constructing the hierarchy
shown in Figure 1.4 from three distinct file systems. The root file system
contains /bin, /home, /etc, and /usr. A file system containing the directories /pal and /robm is spliced onto the directory /home. A second
file system containing the directories /bin, /include, and /include/sys
is spliced onto the directory /usr.

A directory where a file system is attached to the root file system is
usually empty. Its sole purpose is to provide a place to attach another file

system. When the splice occurs and it is replaced, its files and descendant directories (if any) are replaced by the files and descendant directories of the attached file system. However, these files and directories are not destroyed—they are simply unaccessible until the attached file system is removed.

1.4.6 Access Protection

Unix grants or denies access to a file based on the relationship that exists between the file and a user attempting to access it. There are three possible relationships:

1. The user may be the file's *owner*.

2. The user may be a member of the *group* associated with the file.

3. The user may be unrelated to the file. Users unrelated to a file are considered members of the general *public*.

Each time a user attempts to access a file, he or she is treated as the file's owner, a member of the file's group, or a member of the general public. Each file has separate access rights for each of these user classes. These rights, called *permissions*, indicate whether a member of the associated class is allowed to *read*, *write*, or *execute* the file. A particular access right is either granted or denied. All the following eight permutations, called the file's *access modes*, are supported:

- All permissions denied

- Read allowed (called read only)

- Write only

- Read and write allowed

- Execute only

- Read and execute allowed

- Write and execute allowed

- Read, write, and execute allowed

Each user is identified by a unique integer called a *user ID.* Users are also assigned to groups identified by a separate *group ID.* Group members usually have something in common, such as working on a common project or attending the same class. The group called *other* is the default group for users who are not assigned to a specific group.

Each file is assigned an owner and a group when it is created. A file's owner is generally the user who created it. A file's group is usually the owner's group, that is, files are generally assigned to the same group as their owners. However, these assignments can be changed.

When a user accesses a file, that is, attempts to read, write or execute a file, the system compares the user ID of the file's owner with the ID of the user attempting to access it. If the IDs are the same, the user is granted the owner's access rights. Otherwise, Unix compares the user's group ID with the file's group ID. If they match, the user is accorded the group's access rights. Otherwise, the user is allowed the public access rights. For ordinary files:

- Read allows the user to read the file's content. Read permission is also required to copy a file.

- Write allows a user to alter the file's content. Write access is required to overwrite a file.

- Execute allows execution of the file. Since Unix does not distinguish between executable programs and other types of files, execute permission may be granted whether or not the file is a program.

For directories:

- Read allows the user to list the directory's entries.

- Write allows the user to modify a directory's content. Write permission is required to create entries in and remove entries from a directory.

- Execute permits use of the directory within a pathname.

For special files:

- Read permits input from the associated device.

- Write allows output to the associated device.

- Execute has no meaning.

A file's access mode does not affect its owner's ability to change its permissions, its group, or its owner. A file's owner can always change its access mode, its group, and its owner—even when all permissions are denied. However, if a file's owner assigns the file to another user, only the new owner can exercise these privileges. A file's owner cannot change its ownership and then reverse the process.

Section 2.7.1 describes how to determine a file's access mode, and Section 2.7.9 demonstrates how to modify permissions values.

1.5   The Unix Process

A *process* is an instance of a program executing under a Unix operating system. This section describes the relationship between programs and processes, how processes are created, how programs and processes are identified, and the standard I/O streams. The Unix kernel is also discussed briefly. A detailed description of the kernel is more appropriate for a text on Unix internals or operating system theory.

1.5.1   Programs and Processes

A *program* is any file that is executable by the operating system. Programs are sequences of instructions, in one form or another, that carry out a specific task. There are two forms of programs under Unix—*binary executables* and *command language scripts*, or *shell scripts*. Binary executables, also called *executables*, are programs whose instructions are in machine-code form. These programs are compiled from a high-level source language such as C and executed directly by the CPU. Command language scripts are programs whose instructions are sequences of Unix commands and command processor programming constructs. These programs are text files executed on an interpreted basis by the command processor. Regardless of form, programs are static entities, sitting on the file system waiting to be executed.

A *process* is an instance of a running binary executable program. The invocation of a binary executable program typically gives rise to one process. The execution of a shell script usually results in the creation of a sequence of processes—one copy of the command processor to interpret the script and one process for each Unix command that is executed from it. Each process is a dynamic, semi-independent entity. Unix assigns a separate region of memory for program data to each process. However, each process instance of a particular program shares the same text space, that is, regions of executable code, with every other instance of the same program.

Each user may run multiple programs simultaneously, that is, each user may create more than one process. In general, each process associated with a particular user is an instance of a unique program. However, a user may simultaneously run multiple instances of the same program. Each invocation of a program merely creates another process. For example, it is common for a programmer to compile multiple source code files all at the same time.

Unix gives the appearance that users compete with one other for certain system resources, most notably CPU time. System performance apparently degrades in proportion to the number of users logged on to the system. In fact, it is processes that compete for CPU time and other system resources. As the number of users increases, so does the number of processes—thus the decrease in system performance. Of course a single user can dramatically affect system performance by invoking a large number of processes at the same time. Regardless of the number of active users, all processes compete with one another—even processes associated with the same user. Unix attempts to resolve this competition in such a way that each process receives a fair share of the system's resources. While not always successful, each user is generally provided with a uniform level of system performance.

1.5.2   Process Creation and Process Hierarchies

In general, programs are invoked in two steps:

1. A process is created.

2. The program is loaded into memory and executed.

A new process is created by duplicating an existing process. Unix provides a service routine, **fork**, that creates a new process by making a copy of the calling process. That is, when a process calls **fork**, Unix duplicates it and thus creates a new process. Parent/child conventions are used to identify and separate the two processes following the **fork** call—the process that called **fork** is the parent; the new process is its child. Each process learns its identity when the **fork** system call returns. The **fork** call returns different values to the two processes. The parent and child usually key on these values to follow different courses of action. The child normally invokes a new program. The parent usually waits for the child to run its course before continuing.

To load and execute a program, a process calls **exec**—another system routine. The pathname of the desired program and a list of options/command arguments (if any) are passed on the **exec** call. Unix overlays the process calling **exec** with the specified program and thus the new program is executed. In other words, a process that calls **exec** is transformed into an instance of the specified program.

The Unix command processor (described in Section 1.6) utilizes this *fork and exec* sequence to execute command programs. The command processor reads a user command and spawns a child—a copy of itself. The child process then **exec**s the command program while the parent processor, that is, the original shell, waits for the child to exit. Upon the child's exit, the command processor reads the next command and repeats the sequence.

Process hierarchies evolve in a fashion similar to the evolution of a directory hierarchy. A process invokes a child—the child invokes a child of its own, a grandchild of the original process, and so forth. Although there are no constraints on the number of generations in a process hierarchy, process hierarchies are typically fairly shallow—three or perhaps four generations.

1.5.3 Program and Process Identifiers

A program is identified by a pathname since it is merely another ordinary file. A process is identified by a unique integer called a *process ID* or *PID*, assigned by Unix when the process is created. Processes are referred to by their PIDs since the associated program name is not guaranteed to be unique among all processes. In fact the converse is the case. Some programs, such as the command processor, frequently have multiple process instances running at the same time. Section 2.3.6 illustrates the use of PIDs and the difference between a PID and a program name.

1.5.4 Input and Output Data Streams

An important benefit of handling device I/O via the file system's special files is that a program's *I/O data streams* are handled as files. The I/O service routines used to read data from and write data to a disk file are also used to read keystrokes from a keyboard and write output to a display screen. Each process may open, read from, and write to as many as 20 files. Each such file may be unique but this is not essential—a process may open a particular file more than once.

When the command processor invokes a program, the resulting child process generally inherits three open files—*standard input, standard output*, and *standard error*. Standard input is usually associated with the user's terminal keyboard; standard output and error are similarly associated with the display screen. Figure 1.9 illustrates the typical arrangement of standard input, output, and error. Some programs use these files without alteration to interact with users and other programs. Other programs, especially non-interactive programs, modify standard input, output, and

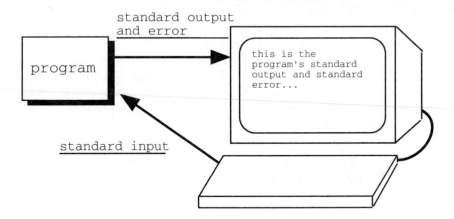

Figure 1.9: Standard input, output, and error

error as necessary to suit their purpose. Many such programs close one or more of these files during initialization.

1.5.5   The Kernel

The core of the Unix operating system, the *kernel*, is not directly visible or accessible to system users. Instead, users interact with the kernel via the command processor and user commands. Many user commands are separate stand-alone programs, sometimes called *command programs*, that are constructed using services provided by the kernel. The kernel contains service routines that create and manage processes, access and manipulate the file system, manage the system's resources, and so forth. Logic is imbedded in these routines, often called *system calls* or *kernel calls*, to insure that resources are properly allocated and CPU time is distributed fairly. In a sense, application programs stimulate the system's administrative and resource management functions each time they call a kernel routine.

Certain system functions, such as process scheduling and memory management, are carried out by separate system processes. These processes vary somewhat from system to system, and the details are unimportant at this point. Readers only need to know that such processes exist because they may encounter them during their experiences with Unix.

1.6   The Unix Command Processor

The Unix command processor is called the *shell*. The shell carries out the mission of any command processor—read, parse, and execute user commands. There are three common shells—the Bourne, C, and Korn shells.

The original, and perhaps most common, is the Bourne shell—**sh** (named for its author). The Bourne shell is available for most Unix systems and is considered by many to be the standard Unix shell. **rsh**, the restricted shell, contains a subset of the Bourne shell's features and provides a user with limited access to a Unix system. **rsh** does not allow certain operations such as changing directories.

The C shell, **csh**, was developed to improve upon the Bourne shell's interactive features. Similarly, the Korn shell, **ksh**, (also named for its author), was designed to enhance the features of the Bourne shell while retaining the C shell's interactive improvements.

Although each shell has its strengths and weaknesses, all three shells are based on the same principles and provide similar fundamental capabilities. This text focuses on the Bourne shell since it is the most common and it is provided with all Unix System V releases. Henceforth, unless otherwise specified, the term *shell* refers to the Bourne shell.

The shell is itself an executable program. Unix invokes a separate instance of the shell for users as they log in (logging in is described Section 2.1). The shell's standard input is read from the user's keyboard. Its standard output and standard error are directed to the user's display. Commands are passed to the shell by the terminal driver. The driver reads characters from the keyboard one at a time. Each character is echoed back to the display and stored in a line buffer. Characters typed by the user are collected in the buffer until a newline or carriage return is typed. Once the newline is typed, the entire line is passed to the shell. The shell parses the command, executes it, and waits for the next one. This read, parse, and execute sequence continues in a loop until the user logs off.

To log off, the user can issue an **exit** command or type <CTRL-d>. **exit** is an explicit instruction to the shell to stop processing. This terminates the user's session since the user is exiting from the command processor. <CTRL-d> signifies the end of the user's input. Since additional commands are not forthcoming, the shell has nothing to do but exit. This effectively terminates the user's session as well.

1.6.1   General Command Syntax

The general syntax of a Unix command is:

name [*-option...*]   [*cmdarg...*]

- *name* is the name of an executable program, an internal shell command, or a pathname that refers to an executable program.

- *option* is generally a single letter, usually preceded by a minus sign (-). However, some options are multiple letters, some are preceded by a plus sign (+), and some stand alone without any preceding character. Options are used to modify or specialize the behavior of the command. In many cases, an option letter is followed by a character string that provides additional information pertaining to the particular option. Option letters that are not followed by a qualifying string may be appended together following a single -.

- *cmdarg* (command argument) is a pathname or some other parameter to be used during the execution of the command.

- [ ] (brackets) enclose *options* and/or *cmdargs* that are optional.

- ... indicates that one or more occurrences of *options* and/or *cmdargs* are allowed.

A complete explanation of the general syntax is contained on the INTRO(1) page in the COMMANDS(1) section of the Unix User's Reference Manual.

The following commands demonstrate typical command syntax. The use of these commands is explained in Chapter 2.

The **cal** command prints calendars:

```
cal [ [ month ] year ]
```

The format indicates that **cal** can be issued without arguments:

```
cal
```

or with a single argument that represents a *year* value:

```
cal 92
```

or with two arguments representing a *month* value followed by a *year* value:

```
cal 6 92
```

Note the sequence of the enclosing brackets and the meaning behind it. The user may specify a year without a month but not a month without a year. A month value is allowed only when a year value is present following it.

The **ls** command prints directory listings; that is, it prints the contents of a given directory or list of directories. Its syntax is:

```
ls [-RadCxmlnogrtucpFbqisf] [pathnames ...]
```

The syntax indicates that **ls** can be issued without options or arguments:

```
ls
```

or with one or more of a host of options, including:

```
ls -a
```

```
ls -Ra
```

```
ls -RdC
```

and so on. It is also valid with one or more *pathnames* or with both *options* and *pathnames*:

```
ls /usr/robm
```

```
ls -a /usr/robm
```

```
ls -al /usr/robm /usr/pal
```

Options, if specified, must precede pathnames.

One drawback of Unix is a lack of consistency in specifying *options* and *cmdargs*. Most Unix commands are stand-alone programs that were developed at different times by different programmers. Syntax guidelines were followed to varying degrees, at times with more success than others. Furthermore, the name of a command does not always indicate its purpose and it is not intended to do so. For some commands, such as **sort**, the purpose is apparent from the command's name. For others, such as **awk**, the purpose is completely obscure. Most users refer to the user's manual frequently until they are familiar with both the purpose and syntax of the most frequently used commands. Commands that are used infrequently send even experienced users to the manual. There are many commands for which the authors still refer to the manual and probably always will.

1.6.2   Correcting Typing Mistakes

The terminal driver recognizes two special characters, called the *erase* and *kill* characters, to correct typing mistakes. The erase character deletes one character from the line buffer. Multiple erase characters delete multiple characters, one for each erase character typed. A user may erase any number of characters up to and including the complete content of the line buffer. The kill character deletes the entire content of the buffer, making it as if the user had typed nothing since the last newline.

The default erase and kill characters are **#** and **@** respectively. The terminal line driver provides a means of changing these character assignments, which is demonstrated in section 2.5. Most users prefer the backspace instead of **#** for the erase character and in some installations this is done automatically. The kill character is usually unchanged.

1.6.3   Additional Shell Features

The shell provides a number of additional features that are designed to enhance its utility and the productivity of its users.

1.6.3.1   Shell and Environment Variables

Shell variables are name-value pairs that provide a mechanism for specifying operational parameters to the shell and other Unix processes. The following examples describe two of the most frequently used shell variables.

Example 1.6 *The* TERM *variable identifies the user's terminal type. Many programs use the value of* TERM *to correctly handle full screen operations.*

Example 1.7 *The* PATH *variable contains a list of directories that are searched by the shell for executable programs. A user command that does not match an internal command or a program in any of these directories cannot be executed unless it is specified by a full pathname. A user can modify the scope and sequence of directories searched for programs simply by modifying the value of* PATH.

The *environment* is a subset of the shell's variables that is passed to each program invoked by the shell. Many programs search the environment for particular variables that contain operational and configuration parameters of interest to them. Creating shell variables, adding variables to the environment, and `TERM` and `PATH` are discussed in Section 2.4.

1.6.3.2 File Name Patterns

A *file name pattern* is a character string, including meta-characters, that the shell treats as representative of a set of potential pathnames instead of as a literal pathname. The shell expands a file name pattern into the list of all file names that both satisfy the pattern and refer to a valid file. In other words, of all possible pathnames that satisfy the pattern, only those pathnames that refer to an existing directory or file appear in the resulting list. File name patterns are useful for identifying or referring to groups of files that meet certain naming criteria. Section 2.6 describes and demonstrates the use of file name patterns.

1.6.3.3 I/O Redirection and Pipelines

One of the original design goals for Unix was to create an environment that encouraged the development of reusable programs. Such programs were envisioned as compact and highly modular building blocks from which more complicated processes would be assembled. The shell provides two means of realizing this goal—*I/O redirection* and *pipelines.*

I/O redirection is a command line mechanism for redefining standard input, output, and error. A user can alter a program's I/O behavior by giving appropriate instructions to the shell. For instance, a user can direct standard output to a file or, as depicted in Figure 1.10, to a printer instead of to the screen. I/O redirection is a temporary modification that has no effect on the program itself, only on a given process instance. Section 2.9.3 explains I/O redirection.

A pipeline is a sequence of commands separated by pipe characters (|). On execution, illustrated in Figure 1.11, the shell directs the standard output of each command into the standard input of the subsequent command. As shown in the example, the output of `1st command` becomes the input of `2nd command`, the output of `2nd command` becomes the input of `3rd command`, and so forth. The output of the whole pipeline is the standard output of the last command in the sequence, in this case `3rd command`. Pipelines are commonly used to create complex processes by combining several simple commands. Section 2.9.4 and the sections that follow it contain some example pipelines.

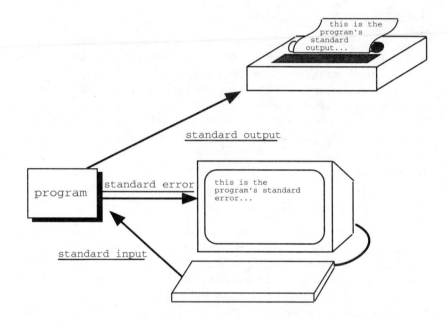

Figure 1.10: Redirecting standard output to a printer

Figure 1.11: A Unix pipeline

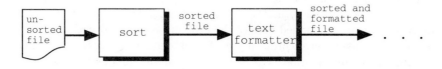

Figure 1.12: A typical pipeline using **sort**

Unix features a number of command programs that take advantage of this concept. Such programs, usually called *filters*, transform their standard input onto their standard output.

Example 1.8 sort *is a general-purpose sorting filter (described in Section 2.10.7). As its name implies,* **sort** *sorts its standard input data stream and sends the result to its standard output.*

While **sort** is capable of handling very complex sorting tasks, its output capability is very limited. Fortunately, there are other filters that are well suited to tasks such as formatting and printing data streams. Filters, like **sort**, are frequently used in pipelines to carry out complex operations. Figure 1.12 depicts a typical pipeline using **sort**. An unsorted file is input to the **sort** command. Its output, the sorted text file, is input to a text formatter. The output of the entire pipeline is a sorted and formatted text file.

1.6.3.4 Shell Scripts

The shell includes a number of structured programming constructs such as loops and conditional branches. A *shell script* or *shell program* is typically a mixture of Unix commands and shell programming constructs contained in a text file. Shell scripts are executed by the shell as if a user had typed the sequence at a keyboard. Such programs can be quite sophisticated—the shell's programming constructs combined with other Unix features constitute a unique high-level language. A proper treatment of shell programming is not essential to the new user and beyond the scope of this text. Readers interested in a more comprehensive treatment are referred to the texts listed in the bibliography.

1.7   The User Account

A *user account* consists of a login name, a password, a home directory, and some administrative files.

A user's *login name*, sometimes called *login ID* or just *login*, identifies an individual as an authorized user of the system. Associated with the login name is the user's password, choice of shell, home directory, and other administrative information. On most Unix systems, users have their own separate accounts. Allowing multiple individuals to access a system using a common login name is usually discouraged as a security risk. However in certain circumstances, a shared login is advantageous.

Each user is assigned a *home directory*. Home directories are traditionally located in the /usr directory but this practice is becoming less commonplace in favor of the /home directory. A separate home directory is normally created for each account. Most users organize files by building a substantial set of subdirectories under their home directory. In a sense, a user's home directory is the root of his or her own directory hierarchy. The structure of this hierarchy is determined by the individual, although some projects or work groups have standards that require the use of a specific structure.

The home directory also contains files used for certain administrative functions. These files are installed and initialized when the account is created or as needed.

Example 1.9 .lastlogin *contains the most recent date and time that the user logged in.*

Example 1.10 .newstime *contains the most recent date and time that the user read the system news. System news is a collection of notices posted by the system administrator. A user is informed that news is available when the current notices are more recent than the date and time contained in* .newstime.

The most important of these administrative files is the user's login profile. This file, named .profile,[3] is a shell script that is executed as the last step of the login process. A user's profile typically initializes the shell's variables, the environment, the terminal type, and the terminal driver's options and control characters. The PATH variable is usually set according to the user's needs, and the erase character is often changed to the backspace character (<CTRL-h>). .profile is also an area where users exercise their own preferences. Since the profile is merely a shell script, users can modify it

---

[3]The term .profile is pronounced "dot-profile."

to their liking. The `.profile` provided to new accounts is usually a standard profile without many bells and whistles. Readers are encouraged to seek out the system administrator or Unix veterans for suggestions regarding their profiles. Project teams and work groups may also define certain requirements for their member's profiles.

1.7.1 User and Group IDs

Recall from the description of the file system that access to files and directories depends on user and group IDs. Upon creation of a new account, each user is assigned a user ID and group ID.

1.8 The System Administrator

The *system administrator* is responsible for the operation of a Unix system. Depending on the size of the installation, the administrator may be an individual or a group of individuals who share the responsibility. The many duties of an administrator include:

- Installing and maintaining software packages

- Configuring and maintaining the system's file system

- Creating and managing user accounts

- Supporting the user community

- Backing up and restoring file systems

- Correcting operational problems

To accomplish these tasks, the system administrator exercises the omnipotent authority of the *super user*. Super users can perform any operation they desire, such as change the system's configuration, override or change the access mode of any file, change user passwords, and activate and deactivate file systems. It is a necessary evil that the super user has enough authority to clobber the entire system. For this reason, special attention is devoted to protecting super user accounts.

1.9 Security

The primary Unix security feature is the user password. On any reasonably administered system, users must supply their password each time they attempt to log in. The purpose of demanding passwords during the login process is to verify the identity of every individual attempting to access the system. The degree of success in preventing unauthorized access is directly related to the vigilance of the system's administrator and its users in selecting and protecting user passwords. Many system invasions occur because an intruder learned someone's password or discovered a login account that was not protected by a password.

The system administrator generally assigns a password to each user when the user's account is created. Thereafter, it is the user's responsibility to select and maintain his or her own password. Section 2.2 describes how to change a user's password.

According to System V specifications, a proper password consists of at least six characters. Two or more of the six characters must be alphabetic and at least one must be a numeric or a special character. Special characters include punctuation marks, the dollar sign, the ampersand, and so on. A user's password cannot be the user's login name or a reversal or circular shift of the user's login name. When comparing potential passwords with the user's login name, upper- and lowercase characters are considered identical. These constraints are intended to encourage users to select passwords that will make penetration of the system difficult. As a general practice, a user should select a password that will be easy to remember without writing it down. The value of any password is somewhat negated if you must write it down to remember it. It is as true in real life as in movies that systems are compromised by written passwords. Random passwords are difficult to penetrate but they can be hard for users to recall as well. Users should choose a topic, name, or other word that has some private meaning for them. After selecting a password, alter its spelling by mixing uppercase with lowercase and replace portions of it with numeric and special characters. Users should avoid words that are associated with them in a well known way or might otherwise be subject to common sense guessing. Poor passwords include a user's name, the names of members of the user's family, the user's birthday, hot current events or news topics, words in the dictionary, and so forth. Users can best protect the system and their accounts by choosing a good password and **keeping it private**. Except for common logins, passwords should not be shared with other users.

Forgotten passwords can be resolved by the system administrator. The administrator can assign a new password to any account. However, the administrator cannot determine the forgotten password. The system does not reveal passwords even to the administrator.

Many installations employ password aging as an additional security precaution. With password aging, the system forces users to change their passwords at regular intervals. For example, users may be required to change their passwords every 90 days. It is also general practice for administrators to create new accounts such that users must change their passwords when they first log in.

Related to passwords are precautions regarding logging off. Users should log off and turn off the terminal whenever they are not actively working on the system, especially if they leave their work area. This protects the system from penetration through an idle terminal. Furthermore, never log in to an idle terminal. One method of penetrating a system is to leave a *trojan horse* login program running on an idle terminal. A trojan horse looks very much like the standard login process. However, it records the user's password for the benefit of an intruder. In this fashion, an intruder attempting to penetrate the system or a user's account obtains a user's password.

File and directory access permissions also provide a form of security by preventing unauthorized access to individual files. However, it is more difficult to penetrate a password than the access permissions.

Another file-level security feature is encryption. Encrypted text files are altered such that they cannot be read. The encryption process uses a code or key defined by the file's owner. Once a file is encrypted, it cannot be decrypted to a usable form without the key.

1.10 Exercises

1. List the relative pathnames for the /bin and /usr/bin directories depicted in Figure 1.4 assuming the following:

   (a) the current directory is /usr

   (b) the current directory is /home/robm

   (c) the current directory is /usr/include/sys

2. All files in the current directory have at least three relative pathnames. Explain.

3. In what directory do files have exactly three relative pathnames?

4. For each of the following statements regarding ordinary and special files, indicate whether the statement is true or false and explain:

   (a) A file may have multiple names within a directory.

   (b) A file may have multiple names within a file system.

   (c) A file may have multiple names on multiple file systems.

5. For each of the following statements regarding directories, indicate whether the statement is true or false and explain:

    (a) A directory may have multiple names within a directory.

    (b) A directory may have multiple names within a file system.

    (c) A directory may have multiple names on multiple file systems.

6. Directories frequently have high link counts. Explain.

7. A file's owner can read and alter the contents of a file that has all permissions denied. Explain.

8. A user can destroy a file but be unable to delete it from the directory. Explain.

9. A user is unable to list the contents of a directory but can execute a program contained in it. Explain.

10. Assuming the erase and kill characters have their default values, what does the line buffer contain if the user types each of the following:

    (a) `helloth## wu#orld<CR>`

    (b) `goodnight sweet @#prince of tides<CR>`

11. Explain how the shell can redirect the output and input streams as well as synchronize the commands in a pipeline.

12. List six "good" passwords and six "bad" passwords.

Chapter 2

Essential Unix Commands

This chapter describes how to log in to and out of a Unix system, how to configure the shell, and how to set the terminal line driver. It also presents some essential Unix commands. The last two sections deal with some of the advanced Unix concepts and commands.

2.1   Logging On and Off a Unix System

To log in to a Unix system, you will need a user account, a full duplex ASCII terminal (visual display and keyboard) or terminal emulator, and a connection to the system. A desktop computer or workstation has a visual display and keyboard connected directly to the computer. However, in many installations, user terminals are connected to the computer by a telecommunications link. Regardless of the details, the system administrator will create your account, provide you with a login name and password, and guide you in regard to connecting to the system. The examples in this section demonstrate logging in once a connection has been established. They do not describe how to establish a connection.

2.1.1   Logging In

Once a connection is established, the system issues the *login prompt*. A typical login prompt looks like the following:

```
login: _
```

The prompt may be preceded by a greeting, a message, a set of instructions, a warning against tampering, and so forth. In any case, the login prompt will be the last item displayed on the terminal. In response, you should type your login name and press the carriage return key[1]. After that, the system issues a *password prompt* similar to the following:

```
Password: _
```

You should respond with your assigned password and press the carriage return key.

The following examples depict a typical login sequence. For these examples, suppose your login name is `pal` and your password is `unix4u!`. The system issues the login prompt and accepts your login name:

```
login: pal<CR>
```

---

[1]A carriage return is depicted here and throughout the text as <CR>.

Bear in mind that Unix distinguishes between upper- and lowercase. You must type your login name exactly as the administrator specified.

Example 2.1 *Pal, PAL, and pal are all distinct login names.*

Following the login prompt and your reply, the system issues the password prompt:

```
login: pal<CR>
Password:
```

In response, type your password. Like the login name, your password must be typed exactly as the system administrator specified. The correct response in this example is `unix4u!` followed by a carriage return. However, the password is not displayed as you type it. This is a security precaution to prevent others from seeing your password as you log in.

If the login name is invalid or the password is not correct, the system indicates that the login failed and reissues the login prompt. The system does not indicate why the login failed—this too is a security precaution. A failed login looks like the following:

```
login: pal<CR>
Password:
login incorrect
login: _
```

If you cannot remember your password or cannot successfully log in, contact the system administrator. The administrator can verify your login name and, if necessary, change your password. The system does not reveal passwords to anyone including the administrator. If you forget your password, changing it is the only option.

A Unix system generally issues some sort of welcome message following a successful login. This message typically identifies the Unix version and applicable copyrights, specifies the system's *node name*, indicates when *news* is available, and informs you if you have *mail*. The system's node name is a symbolic name or address by which the system is known to other systems on a network. News are messages posted by the system administrator for the user's convenience. Mail is electronic messages sent from one user to another. News and mail are similar except that news is addressed to all users and mail is addressed to specific users.

High-priority notices are often issued automatically following the login sequence. In the following example, the system's node name is `blakhole` and the system administrator posted a notice that the system will be down for maintenance. Also note that there is no news, but the user has mail:

```
AT&T UNIX System V Release 4.0
Copyright (c) 1984, 1986, 1987, 1988, 1989, 1990 AT&T
All Rights Reserved
blakhole
Last login: Sun Jan 26 17:56:19 on tty01

The system will be down today from 5:45 PM to 6:45 PM
for routine maintenance.

you have mail.

$ _
```

The system issues the *command prompt* following the welcome screen. The command prompt indicates that the shell is ready and waiting. The default prompt is the dollar sign character (**$**).

2.1.2   Correcting Typing Errors While Logging In

You must use the system's default erase (**#**) and kill (**@**) characters to correct typing errors while logging in. These characters cannot be changed until after you log in unless they are changed in the login profile.

An *erase character* nullifies the character preceding it. Multiple erase characters are cumulative—one character is deleted for each erase character typed. However, once enough erase characters are typed to cancel the entire input line, additional erase characters have no further effect.

A *kill character* nullifies the entire input line. Following a kill character, the system behaves as if you had typed nothing at all. Multiple kill characters have no practical effect since each one following the first merely deletes an empty line.

Suppose in the previous example you incorrectly typed **pat** instead of **pal** while logging in. The error is easily corrected with the erase character as follows:

```
login: pat#l<CR>
Password: _
```

Or the entire line can be deleted with the kill character and typed correctly:

```
login: pat@
pal<CR>
Password: _
```

Correcting login name errors with the erase character is easier than correcting password errors. Login name errors are visible—password errors are not. The simplest way to correct a password error is to type the kill character and start over.

2.1.3 Logging Out

Log out whenever you are not actively using the system, especially if you leave the area where the terminal is located. Logging out is accomplished by issuing the **exit** command or by typing <CTRL-d> (<CTRL-d> is not visible as it is typed—it is depicted in the examples for the benefit of the reader). Either method is generally acceptable.

  exit is a shell command so it must be followed by a carriage return:

```
$ exit<CR>
```

<CTRL-d> is handled by the terminal line driver so it need not be followed by a carriage return:

```
$ <CTRL-d>
```

  Unless you break the connection to the system after logging out, the system re-initiates the login sequence and issues a login prompt:

```
$ exit<CR>

Welcome to the AT&T 386 UNIX System
System name: blakhole

login: _
```

You can also effectively log out by breaking the terminal's connection to the system. However, this may cause processes to hang (that is, continue to run erroneously) and it can cause files to be mishandled and damaged. Therefore, break the connection to the system only after logging out or when it is the only remaining option for concluding your login session.

2.2 Changing Your Password

The system administrator assigns a password when your account is created. Thereafter, maintaining your password is your responsibility.

  In general, you can change your password whenever you wish with the **passwd** command as follows:

```
$ passwd<CR>
passwd:  Changing password for pal
Old password:
New password:
Re-enter new password:
$ _
```

You must first provide your existing password. If you fail to type your current password correctly, **passwd** halts, leaving your password unchanged:

```
$ passwd<CR>
passwd:  Changing password for pal
Old password:
Sorry.
$ _
```

You must also type your new password twice. If it doesn't meet standards or you fail to type it the same way both times, **passwd** halts without changing your password. You will be allowed several attempts to get the job done:

```
$ passwd
passwd:  Changing password for robm
Old password:
New password:
Re-enter new password:
They don't match; try again.
New password:
Password is too short - must be at least 6 characters
New password:
Re-enter new password:
passwd: Too many tries; try again later
$ _
```

In this example, three unsuccessful attempts were made to change the user's password. Once it failed to meet standards and twice the two copies didn't match.

Many installations employ *password aging*. With password aging, the system periodically requires you to change your password. When it expires, the system prompts you to change it after you log in:

```
login: pal
Password:

AT&T UNIX System V Release 4.0
Copyright (c) 1984, 1986, 1987, 1988, 1989, 1990 AT&T
All Rights Reserved
blakhole
Last login: Sun Jan 26 17:56:19 on tty01

Your password has expired.  Choose a new password.
Old password: _
```

The procedure is the same as invoking **passwd** directly. You must type your expired password followed by a new password twice. Once your password expires, the system prevents you from logging in until it is changed.

Unix never displays passwords, even expired ones. When changing your password, whether at your request or required by the system, your current and new passwords will not be visible. Furthermore, Unix applies additional security measures in an attempt to make sure you actually change the password. Your new password must differ from your old one by at least three characters and differences only in case do not count. That is, changing a particular character from upper- to lowercase or the converse is not considered a change in that character position.

Some installations also employ a feature similar to password aging that prevents you from immediately changing a new password. The system requires that a password reach a certain age before it can be changed by anyone other than the super user. For example, the system may require that passwords be at least two weeks old before they can be changed.

2.3   A Quick Introduction to Unix Commands

This section contains a quick introduction to some of the most commonly used Unix commands. Its purpose is to provide you with a "hands on" look at some of the concepts introduced in the first chapter. Try each command as it is presented and compare your results with the examples in the text. Bear in mind that these examples are necessarily contrived. You may expect similar but not identical results from your system.

A Unix command can be generally halted by pressing the break key or the delete key. The locations of these keys vary from keyboard to keyboard. The break key is occasionally labeled `Brk`—delete is sometimes labeled `Del`. If you become concerned with the behavior of a runaway command and cannot successfully halt it with either of these keys, contact the system administrator.

Each of the commands described in this section are discussed at a cursory level. These and other commands will be discussed at a more deliberate pace and in more detail in the remaining sections of this chapter.

2.3.1   pwd - Print Working Directory

pwd prints the full pathname of the current directory. For example, suppose your login name is `pal` and you have just logged in to the system. **pwd** prints the name of your home directory:

```
$ pwd<CR>
/home/pal
$ _
```

pwd is useful whenever you are unsure of your location in the directory hierarchy.

2.3.2   ls - List Contents of Directory

ls lists the contents of directories. Without options or arguments, **ls** lists the name of each file in the current directory including ordinary and special files as well as other directories. Continuing with the example from the previous section, you can use **ls** to learn the contents of your home directory:

```
$ ls<CR>
$ _
```

This seems like an uninteresting and useless result. However, it demonstrates a characteristic feature of Unix commands—they are typically silent when they have nothing of interest to report. From this example, you may infer that your home directory is empty. However, this is not the case. **ls** does not list files that start with a period character (`.`) unless explicitly asked to do so. The `-a` option[2] instructs **ls** to list all files, including those that start with a period character:

```
$ ls -a<CR>
.
..
.profile
$ _
```

---

[2]This option is pronounced "minus a."

Here we see the two special-purpose files, . and .., and the user's login profile, .profile. The file . refers to the directory that contains it, that is, it refers to /home/pal. The file .. refers to the parent of the directory that contains it, that is, it refers to /home.

ls has options which instruct it to print useful information in addition to file names. For instance, the -p option causes ls to append a slash character (/) to each directory name that appears in its output. You may also provide one or more pathnames as arguments to ls. For each pathname that refers to a directory, ls lists the contents of that directory. For each pathname that refers to an ordinary or special file, ls lists that file along with whatever additional information is called for by command options. Consider the following examples:

```
$ ls -ap .<CR>
./
../
.profile

$ ls -ap ..<CR>
./
../
pal/
robm/

$ ls -p .profile<CR>
.profile
$ _
```

Both the -a and -p options are used with a pathname of . in the first example. ls lists all files in the current directory and appends a slash to the directory names dot (.) and dot-dot (..). A slash is not appended to .profile since it is the name of an ordinary file. The second example applies the same options to the dot-dot directory, that is, to /home—the parent of the current directory. /home contains four directories—dot, dot-dot, pal and robm. The directories dot and dot-dot refer to /home and / respectively. pal we are familiar with. robm is the home directory of another user. In the final example, .profile is passed to ls as a pathname argument. ls lists .profile, but -p has no effect since there are no directory names in the output.

2.3.3   cat - Concatenate and Print Files

cat is commonly used to look at the contents of ASCII text files. To view the contents of the *password file*, try the following example:

```
$ cat /etc/passwd<CR>
root:x:0:1:0000-Admin(0000):/:
daemon:x:1:1:0000-Admin(0000):/:
bin:x:2:2:0000-Admin(0000):/usr/bin:
sys:x:3:3:0000-Admin(0000):/:
adm:x:4:4:0000-Admin(0000):/var/adm:
uucp:x:5:5:0000-uucp(0000):/usr/lib/uucp:
lp:x:7:8:0000-LP(0000):/home/lp:/sbin/sh
service:x:9:9:Service Login:/service:
nuucp:x:10:10:0000-uucp(0000):/var/spool/uucppublic:/usr/lib/uucp/uucico
listen:x:37:4:Network Admin:/usr/net/nls:
sync:x:67:1:0000-Admin(0000):/:/usr/bin/sync
install:x:101:1:Initial Login:/home/install:
robm:x:1000:1:Robert Martin:/home/robm:
pal:x:1001:1:Phil Laplante:/home/pal:
$ _
```

cat outputs the contents of the file, in this case the password file, to the
user's terminal. The password file contains, among other things, the login
name, user name, and home directory of each system user.

  cat prints multiple files if more than one pathname argument is provided:

```
cat file1 file2 ...   fileN<CR>
(contents of file1 appears first)...
(contents of file2 appears second)...
(contents of fileN appears last)...
```

cat prints each file in turn without any break or pause. Since this capability
does not offer a reasonable opportunity to peruse the output, it is more
useful when the output is redirected to a new file or a device such as a
printer.

2.3.4   pg - Page Filter

A better means of perusing files is **pg**, the page filter command. **pg** displays
its output in chunks, called pages, that are no longer than the number of

lines on the screen. **pg** pauses after each page is output, allowing the user an opportunity to read the screen. Users indicate when they are ready to proceed to the next page by pressing the carriage return key.

Unlike **cat**, which presents its output in strict sequential order, **pg** allows the user to move backward through a file as well as forward. Consider the following example:

```
$ pg -5 /etc/passwd<CR>
root:x:0:1:0000-Admin(0000):/:
daemon:x:1:1:0000-Admin(0000):/:
bin:x:2:2:0000-Admin(0000):/usr/bin:
sys:x:3:3:0000-Admin(0000):/:
adm:x:4:4:0000-Admin(0000):/var/adm:
:<CR>
uucp:x:5:5:0000-uucp(0000):/usr/lib/uucp:
lp:x:7:8:0000-LP(0000):/home/lp/sbin/sh
service:x:9:9:Service Login:/service:
nuucp:x:10:10:0000-uucp(0000):/var/spool/uucppublic:/usr/lib/uucp/uucico
:-<CR>
root:x:0:1:0000-Admin(0000):/:
daemon:x:1:1:0000-Admin(0000):/:
bin:x:2:2:0000-Admin(0000):/usr/bin:
sys:x:3:3:0000-Admin(0000):/:
adm:x:4:4:0000-Admin(0000):/var/adm:
:q<CR>
$ _
```

For this example the page length was constrained to five lines with the $-n$ option:

```
$ pg -5 ...
```

where n is an integer value that specifies the desired page length. The default page length depends on the terminal type specified by the TERM variable. In this case the page length was 23 lines so the password file, which is only 14 lines long, could have been displayed in a single page.

To move forward to the next page the user presses a carriage return at the colon prompt (:). To move backward one page the user types a minus sign (-) followed by a carriage return. A user can move backward multiple pages by typing an integer value immediately following the minus sign. For example, the user can move backward two pages by typing -2. To skip forward a number of pages the user types +n, where n is an integer value representing the number of pages to skip ahead.

2.3.5   who - Who is On the System

who lists the users that are logged in to the system:

```
$ who<CR>
pal          console       Feb  2 11:00
robm         tty01         Feb  2 10:45
$ _
```

For each active user, **who** reports the user's login name, the user's *terminal device*, and the date and time that the user logged in. The user's terminal device, frequently called a *tty port*, is an asynchronous input/output port to which the user's terminal is connected. A terminal device is an example of a special file.

who's output is restricted to the user issuing the command as follows:

```
$ who am i<CR>
pal           console       Feb  2 11:00
$ _
```

2.3.6   ps - Process Status Report

ps prints information about running processes. In its simplest form, **ps** produces an abbreviated report of those processes associated with the user issuing the command:

```
$ ps<CR>
   PID TTY       TIME COMD
   401 console   0:00 sh
   402 console   0:00 ps
$ _
```

The columns appearing in this report are defined as follows:

PID is a process ID.

TTY is the terminal device controlling the process.

TIME is the amount of CPU time used by the process since its invocation.

COMD is the command name, that is, the name of the program that gave rise to the reported process.

In this example, **ps** reported the user's shell and **ps** itself. **ps** prints a snapshot of active processes at a given moment in time. The report may not be completely accurate at the time it is printed. On occasion you may find that **ps** doesn't report itself even though it is obviously running.

ps lists processes associated with other users, including system processes, with the -u option:

```
$ ps -u root
   PID TTY        TIME COMD
     0 ?         0:00 sched
     1 ?         0:01 init
     2 ?         0:00 pageout
     3 ?         0:01 fsflush
     4 ?         0:00 kmdaemon
   235 ?         0:00 sac
   217 ?         0:01 lpsched
   210 ?         0:00 rpc.ruse
   231 ?         0:00 cat
   191 ?         0:00 cron
   203 ?         0:00 rpcbind
   208 ?         0:00 rpc.rwal
   212 ?         0:00 rpc.spra
   228 ?         0:00 lpNet
$ _
```

In this example, **ps** reports all processes associated with the *root user*, that is, those processes associated with the system itself. **sched** is the process scheduler. **init** is responsible for starting and monitoring system processes. **pageout** is the memory manager. **lpsched** is the scheduler for the print spooler. The ? appearing in the **TTY** column indicates that the process is not controlled by a particular terminal device.

Additional information is reported when various options are used. For example:

```
$ ps -f -urobm
    UID   PID  PPID  C    STIME TTY       TIME COMD
    robm  236     1  1 20:25:50 console  0:01 sh
    robm  325   236  6 21:03:35 console  0:00 ps -f -urobm
$ _
```

With the -f option:

UID is the user's login name.

PPID is the parent process ID. Note in this example that the shell, PID 236, is the parent of **ps**, PID 325.

STIME is the time the process was started.

COMD is expanded to include arguments in addition to the command name.

2.3.7   mail - Send and Receive Mail

mail is a basic electronic mail facility. In the example welcome screen from Chapter 1, the system informed the user that he or she had mail. The user invokes **mail** without arguments to read the message or messages:

```
$ mail<CR>
From robm Sun Feb  2 11:10 EST 1992
Content-Type: text
Content-Length: 117

Phil,

I would like to get a copy of your notes
for last week's C class.  Please call
me when you can.

Thanks,
Rob
?
```

mail prints the most recently received message, prompts the user with a question mark (?) and awaits the user's response. The user has several options:

r Send a reply. **mail** accepts a reply from the user (typing a message is described below), transmits it to the current message's sender, and then deletes the current message.

file(s) Saves the message in the specified file or files. By default, **mail** saves the message in a file named mbox in the user's home directory.

user(s) Forward the message to the specified user or users. Each receipient is indicated by his or her login name.

d Deletes the message and advances to the next one if it exists.

? Produces a list of the user's options along with a brief explanation of each one.

To send a message, **mail** is invoked with a list of login IDs. **mail** reads a message from the user and sends it to each of the specified receipients. The message from the previous example was sent as follows:

```
$ mail pal<CR>
Phil,<CR>
<CR>
I would like to get a copy of your notes<CR>
for last week's C class.  Please call<CR>
me when you can.<CR>
<CR>
Thanks,<CR>
Rob<CR>
.<CR>
$ _
```

After invoking **mail**, the user simply types the intended message. Each line typed by the user is included in the message. The message is terminated by a line that contains a single period character in the first column.

2.3.8   cal - Print Calendars

As mentioned in Section 1.6.1, **cal** prints calendars:

```
$ cal<CR>
   February 92
 S  M Tu  W Th  F  S
            1  2  3  4
 5  6  7  8  9 10 11
12 13 14 15 16 17 18
19 20 21 22 23 24 25
26 27 28 29

$ _
```

Without arguments, **cal** prints a calendar for the current month and year.

2.4   Shell Variables and the Environment

As discussed previously, *shell variables* are name-value pairs used to pass configuration and operational parameters to the shell and other processes.

Shell variables are also used in a more traditional sense within shell scripts. The *environment* is a subset of the shell's variables that is passed to the shell's child processes.

2.4.1   set - Display Set Variables

The **set** command, without arguments, displays the value of each shell variable:

```
$ set<CR>
HOME=/home/robm
HZ=100
IFS=

LOGNAME=robm
MAIL=/usr/mail/robm
MAILCHECK=600
OPTIND=1
PATH=/usr/bin
TERM=AT386-M
TERMCAP=/etc/termcap
TZ=EST5EDT
$ _
```

These are some of the more common shell variables. `HOME` is the user's home directory and `LOGNAME` is the user's login name. `PATH` is described in Section 2.4.3. `TERM` is described in Section 2.4.4.

2.4.2   Creating and Assigning Shell Variables

Shell variables are created and assigned values using the following assignment statement:

variable_name=value

If *variable_name* is not an existing shell variable, the shell creates it and assigns it the specified *value*. Otherwise, the variable's value is simply replaced. The absence of *whitespace* is important since the shell treats white space as a field separator. Whitespace includes space and tab characters. Attempting an assignment statement with the following syntax:

variable_name = *value*

will produce unexpected results and probably cause an error. The shell attempts to invoke *variable_name* as a command, passing = and *value* as arguments.

PS1 is the system prompt variable. The shell outputs this value to the user each time it is ready to read the next command. Consider the following three examples:

```
$ PS1 = "ready captain > "<CR>
PS1: not found

$ PS1="ready captain > "<CR>

ready captain > PS1="$ "<CR>
$ _
```

The improper syntax in the first example produces the error message:

```
PS1: not found
```

The shell attempts to execute PS1 as a command but can't find the appropriate program file. The second example demonstrates correct syntax. The system prompt is changed to:

```
ready captain >
```

Finally, the system prompt is changed back to its default value.

2.4.3 The PATH Variable

The PATH variable, introduced in Section 1.6.3.1, lists directories that the shell searches for program files when attempting to execute a user's command. Pathnames in the list are separated by colons. The shell searches each directory, in the order specified, until it finds a program file that matches the command name. If a matching file cannot be found, the command cannot be carried out.

In the example depicted in Section 2.4.1, PATH is set to /usr/bin. This means that /usr/bin is the only directory searched for program files. The scope of directories searched for command program files can be expanded by adding additional directories to the PATH variable:

```
$ PATH=$PATH:/usr/ucb<CR>
$ echo $PATH<CR>
/usr/bin:/usr/ucb
$ _
```

The shell treats any string preceded by a $ as a variable name. If the variable exists, the shell substitutes its value in place of the string. Otherwise, the string is removed leaving nothing, or a *null*, in its place. In this example, PATH exists so the string $PATH is replaced by its value, /usr/bin. The shell appends :/usr/ucb to this and assigns /usr/bin:/usr/ucb to the PATH variable. This command produces the same results as:

```
PATH=/usr/bin:/usr/ucb
```

but is more commonly used since it preserves the existing value of PATH without retyping it. The **echo** command, used in this example to display the value of PATH, repeats or echoes its arguments to standard output. This command is frequently used to examine the current value of shell variables.

An empty directory field in the PATH variable, represented by a leading colon, a trailing colon, or two colons directly adjacent to one another (::), indicates that the shell should search the current directory. The current directory is not searched in the PATH examples seen thus far. The following three examples demonstrate various ways to add the current directory to PATH. Assuming the original PATH value of /usr/bin, both the current directory and /usr/ucb can be added to PATH in any of the following ways:

```
$ PATH=:$PATH:/usr/ucb<CR>
$ echo $PATH<CR>
:/usr/bin:/usr/ucb
$ _
```

or

```
$ PATH=$PATH::/usr/ucb<CR>
$ echo $PATH<CR>
/usr/bin::/usr/ucb
$ _
```

or

```
$ PATH=$PATH:/usr/ucb:<CR>
$ echo $PATH<CR>
/usr/bin:/usr/ucb:
$ _
```

The difference between each of these cases is the order in which the directories are searched. In the first case, the current directory is searched first, followed by /usr/bin and finally /usr/ucb. In the second, /usr/bin is searched followed by the current directory and /usr/ucb. In the final example, the current directory is searched last.

2.4.4 The Environment

The *environment* is a subset of the shell's variables that is automatically provided to its child processes. Each time the shell invokes a child process, a copy of the environment is passed to the child. The shell's environment and those of its children are completely separate. A child process can modify its environment, which is a common occurrence, without affecting its parent shell's environment.

One important use of the environment is to identify your terminal type to the system. There are a variety of ASCII terminals and terminal families suitable for use with Unix systems. Many of these terminals use different character sequences to control the cursor and the display. Unix programs that provide a full screen interface or display, notably the visual editor **vi**, employ a screen handling utility that translates generic cursor movement commands into terminal-specific character sequences. This utility relies on the environment variable TERM to identify the user's terminal type. If TERM is not in the environment or has an unrecognized value, the screen handler complains when it is initialized.

Depending on local standards and practices, TERM may or may not be placed in the environment when you login. The **env** command produces a list of the variables contained in the environment:

```
$ env<CR>
HOME=/home/robm
HZ=100
LOGNAME=robm
MAIL=/usr/mail/robm
PATH=/usr/bin:/usr/ucb
TZ=EST5EDT
$ _
```

In this example, TERM is not present. Variables are placed in the environment with the **export** command:

```
$ TERM=vt100<CR>
$ export TERM<CR>
$ env<CR>
HOME=/home/robm
HZ=100
LOGNAME=robm
MAIL=/usr/mail/robm
PATH=/usr/bin:/usr/ucb
TZ=EST5EDT
TERM=vt100
$ _
```

Only environment variables are passed to child processes. All other shell variables are unknown to the shell's children.

It is a common practice for Unix users to set and export many shell variables, especially PATH and TERM, in their login profiles. Some of these variables are system-defined—others are user-defined. As always, if you need help with your profile, seek the assistance of the system administrator or an experienced user.

2.5   The Terminal Driver

The *terminal driver* or *tty driver* manages asynchronous input/output ports, that is, terminal devices. The tty driver controls baud rate, parity checking, number of bits in a character, handshaking, and so forth, and handles all input from and output to the terminal. In general, the terminal driver reads characters one by one as they are typed by the user. Most of these characters are placed directly into a line buffer. However, certain characters, in particular *CTRL-characters*, are recognized by and processed as instructions to the terminal driver. A "CTRL-character" is any character typed in conjunction with the *Ctrl* key. We have already discussed two examples of characters that are recognized and processed by the terminal driver—the erase and kill characters. Depending on the terminal driver's internal settings, the driver may take other actions such as sending a signal to the user's shell process or replacing one character with another.

2.5.1   stty - Set Terminal Driver

The **stty** command allows the user to read and modify the terminal driver's internal settings and control character assignments. Without options, **stty** reports the terminal driver's basic settings:

```
$ stty<CR>
speed 9600 baud; evenp
erase = ^h; swtch = <undef>; dsusp = <undef>;
brkint -inpck icrnl onlcr tab3
echo echoe echok
$ _
```

Some of the settings and control characters in this example are defined as follows:

speed 9600 baud The baud rate is set to 9600.

        evenp Parity checking is set for even parity. Odd parity checking is indicated by oddp.

erase = ^ h: the erase character is CTRL-h, the backspace character.

     brkint On a break key, an *interrupt* signal is sent to the process reading from standard input.

    -inpck Input parity checking is disabled. If parity checking was enabled it would be indicated by inpck.

     icrnl Map carriage return characters to newline characters, that is, replace all carriage returns with newlines.

      echo Echo all typed characters back to the terminal.

    echoe Echo erase characters. This causes erase characters to be mapped to a "backspace, space, backspace" sequence that erases the deleted character from the screen.

    echok Outputs a newline character when the kill character is typed.

This example does not include all of the terminal driver's options and control characters. Note that the kill character is not listed. The -a option causes **stty** to report all settings and options:

```
$ stty -a<CR>
speed 9600 baud;
intr = DEL; quit = ^|; erase = ^h; kill = @;
eof = ^d; eol = <undef>; eol2 = <undef>; swtch = <undef>;
start = ^q; stop = ^s; susp = ^z; dsusp = <undef>;
rprnt = ^r; flush = ^o; werase = ^w; lnext = ^v;
parenb -parodd cs8 -cstopb -hupcl cread -clocal -loblk -parext
-ignbrk brkint ignpar -parmrk -inpck istrip -inlcr -igncr icrnl -iuclc
ixon ixany -ixoff -imaxbel
isig icanon -xcase echo echoe echok -echonl -noflsh
-tostop -echoctl -echoprt -echoke -defecho -flusho -pendin -iexten
opost -olcuc onlcr -ocrnl -onocr -onlret -ofill -ofdel tab3
$ _
```

Here you can see that the kill character (end of the second line) is assigned
the default value. The other control characters and settings in this example
are explained in the User's Reference Manual (see Appendix B).

To set the value for a control character, invoke **stty** with the following
syntax:

stty *control-character value*

where *control-character* is one of the terminal driver's control character
symbols, such as **kill** or **erase**, and *value* is the desired value. To assign
an ordinary character to a terminal driver control character, simply type it
following the control character's symbol:

```
$ stty erase q<CR>
$ stty
speed 9600 baud; evenp
erase = q; swtch = <undef>; dsusp = <undef>;
brkint -inpck icrnl onlcr tab3
echo echoe echok
```

In this example, q is assigned as the terminal driver's erase character. Each
time the user types a q the previous character is deleted. This is admittedly a contrived example—very few users would want q to be the erase
character. However, its purpose is to illustrate the difference between assigning ordinary characters and CTRL-characters to terminal driver control
characters. A CTRL-character is assigned as follows:

```
$ stty erase \^h<CR>
$ _
```

or

```
$ stty erase '^h'<CR>
$ _
```

Both of these examples assign the backspace key (`<CTRL-h>`) as the erase character—the only difference between the two is syntax. The user typed a caret (`^`) followed by an **h** to represent the backspace key (`<CTRL-h>`). The caret (`^`), like the dollar sign (`$`), has a special meaning to the shell. This special meaning is suppressed by *escaping* or *quoting* the character. A single character is escaped by preceding it with a backslash character (`\`), as demonstrated in the first example. One or more characters are quoted by enclosing the string in single quote characters (`'`), which was demonstrated in the second example. Assigning a "CTRL-character" to one of the tty driver's control characters must be done as shown in these examples.

To set one of the terminal driver's options, invoke **stty** with the following syntax:

```
stty option
```

where *option* is the terminal driver option to be set or canceled. For example:

```
$ stty -echoe<CR>
$ _
```

stops echo of the erase character and:

```
$ stty echoe<CR>
$ _
```

turns it back on again.

Another useful **stty** option is **sane**. This option is typically used when a user's terminal behaves erratically. Programs crash, especially during development, and experiments with **stty** can go astray leaving the terminal driver in an unusual or unreliable state. If the terminal seems to behave strangely:

```
$ stty sane<CR>
$ _
```

attempts to restore the terminal driver to a more rational condition.

The system administrator may or may not have arranged the terminal driver's control characters and option settings to everyone's liking. If not, issue the appropriate **stty** commands after logging in or add them to your profile.

2.6   File Name Generation

File name generation is a convenient short hand for referring to files and directories as command arguments. The characters *, ?, [, and], when used in command arguments, specify file name patterns. The shell expands these patterns into lists consisting of all file names that both match the pattern and refer to a valid file. The expanded list is passed to the command as its arguments instead of the file name pattern. If the expanded list is empty, i.e., there are no files which match the pattern, the pattern itself is passed.

To examine file name generation, suppose that the following files are contained in the current directory:

- module1.c

- module2.c

- module3.c

- module1.doc

- module2.doc

- module3.doc

The question mark character (?) matches any single character. Therefore, the pattern module?.c is expanded by the shell into the following list:

```
module1.c module2.c module3.c
```

For example:

```
$ echo module?.c<CR>
module1.c module2.c module3.c
$ _
```

Recall that **echo** outputs its arguments back to the terminal. However in this case, the single argument `module?.c` was expanded into the list of file names before the **echo** command was executed. That is, the shell replaced `module?.c` with `module1.c module2.c module3.c` before it invoked the **echo** command.

The asterisk character $(*)^3$ matches any string of characters, including the empty or null string. The previous example could have been typed:

```
$ echo module*.c<CR>
module1.c module2.c module3.c
$ _
```

However, it could also have been typed:

```
$ echo mod*.c
module1.c module2.c module3.c
$ _
```

Finally it could have been typed:

```
$ echo *.c<CR>
module1.c module2.c module3.c
$ _
```

Keep in mind that where `*` matches strings of any length, `?` matches only single characters. Consider the following two examples:

```
$ echo *.*<CR>
module1.c module2.c module3.c module1.doc module2.doc module3.doc
$ echo *.?<CR>
module1.c module2.c module3.c
$ _
```

In the second example, the files ending in `doc` didn't appear because `?` cannot match a three-character string.

File name generation using brackets (`[`, `]`) is slightly more complicated. Brackets specify character classes, that is, groups or ranges of characters which meet certain criteria. A class may be enumerated explicitly, for example:

```
[abcdefghijklmnopqrstuvwxyz]
```

---

[3]This character is sometimes pronounced "star" or "splatt."

This class matches any single lowercase character. Lexical character ranges may be used within a character class specification to save typing. The syntax for a lexical range is:

[l-u]

where l is the lower bound and u is the upper bound. The character range includes l, u, and all characters that are lexically between them. The class of lowercase characters is specified as follows:

[a-z]

and the class of uppercase characters is specified by:

[A-Z]

A character class may contain multiple range specifications. The class of all alphabetic characters is specified by:

[a-zA-Z]

Character classes match single characters in a fashion similar to ?. To examine character classes, let us add the following to the list of file names:

- modulea.c

- moduleb.c

- modulec.c

and consider the following examples:

```
$ echo *[a-z].c<CR>
modulea.c moduleb.c modulec.c
$ echo *[0-9].c<CR>
module1.c module2.c module3.c
$ echo *[ab12].c<CR>
modulea.c moduleb.c module1.c module2.c
$ echo *[!0-9].c<CR>
modulea.c moduleb.c module3.c
$ echo *[A-Z].c<CR>
*[A-Z].c
$ _
```

Of note in these examples:

- The class of numeric characters is specified by [0-9].

- [ab12] is an explicit class consisting of a, b, 1 and 2.

- Within a character class the exclamation point (!)[4] negates or complements the class. That is, the pattern matches any character except those characters within the class.

- In the final example, the file name pattern failed to match a file. Therefore, the file name pattern is passed to the **echo** command unchanged.

File name patterns are used frequently—to move, copy, print, and occasionally delete files; and therefore particularly important to the Unix user. New users are well advised to practice the use of these patterns until they can produce reliable results. Many a file has been lost due to the careless or hurried use of file name patterns. If the reader is ever unsure of what a particular pattern will produce, test the pattern first with the **echo** command to insure it behaves as desired.

2.7 File Commands

In this section, we present commands commonly used to manage ordinary and special files. While these commands frequently apply to directories as well, their use is not limited to directories.

2.7.1 ls - List Contents of Directory

As discussed in Section 2.3.2, **ls** lists the contents of directories. More specifically, it lists the entries contained in a directory along with information pertaining to those entries. In this section, we discuss options and features of **ls** that were not covered in Section 2.3.2.

By default, **ls** lists each entry in lexical order, one to a line:

---

[4]This character is sometimes pronounced "ball-bat" or "bang."

```
$ ls /bin<CR>
STTY
acctcom
ar
at
atq
atrm
awk
backup
banner
basename
batch
.

.

.
ls
mail
.

.

.
ypcat
ypmatch
ypwhich
zcat
$ _
```

Lexical order is not alphabetical order—uppercase characters precede low-ercase characters. Refer to an ASCII table for the lexical order of the ASCII character set. The above listing of the /usr/bin directory is too lengthy to place in the text in its entirety. It is also difficult to read as it flashes by on the terminal. The -C option instructs **ls** to format its output in columns:

```
$ ls -C /usr/bin<CR>
STTY          cut           getpath       mapchan       removepkg     trchan
acctcom       date          getrange      mapkey        restore       true
.
.
.
crontab       getdev        lp            putdgrp       time          ypwhich
csh           getdgrp       lpstat        pwconv        timex         zcat
csplit        getgid        ls            pwd           touch
ct            getint        mail          pwdmenu       tplot
ctags         getkeywd      mailalias     random        tput
cu            getopt        mailx         red           tr
$ _
```

Even in this format the complete listing is too lengthy to place in the text. The −C option orders directory entries vertically down each column. To produce a similar output ordered horizontally across each row:

```
$ ls -x /usr/bin<CR>
STTY       acctcom     ar          at          atq         atrm
awk        backup      banner      basename    batch       bc
bdiff      bfs         cal         calendar    cancel      captoinfo
cat        checkeq     chgrp       chkey       chmod       chown
.
.
.
write      x286        x286emul    xargs       xrestor     xrestore
xtract     xts         xtt         yes         ypcat       ypmatch
ypwhich    zcat
$ _
```

Another useful option for the **ls** command is −F. Similar to the −p option, −F causes **ls** to append a character to certain directory entries appearing in the output. Consider the following:

```
$ ls -C -F /<CR>
altboot*     etc/         install/      opt/        service/     u/
bin@         export/      lib@          proc/       shlib/       unix@
dev/         home/        lost+found/   quotas      stand/       usr/
dgn*         home2/       mnt/          sbin/       tmp/         var/
$ _
```

The characters appended to file names are interpreted as follows:

* The entry refers to an executable program, including both binary executables and shell scripts.

/ The entry refers to a directory.

@ The entry is a soft link to another directory entry.

Entries that refer to special files or to ordinary files that are not executable appear as they always have.

Perhaps one of the most often used options is -l. This option produces the *long listing* format:

```
$ ls -l /<CR>
total 70
-r-xr-xr-x    2 root       root          1476 Oct 16  1990 altboot
lrwxrwxrwx    1 bin        bin              8 Oct 16  1990 bin -> /usr/bin
drwxrwxr-x   13 root       sys           4608 Jun  6 20:34 dev
-r-xr-xr-x    2 root       root          1476 Oct 16  1990 dgn
drwxrwxr-x   27 root       sys           3072 Jun  7 08:24 etc
drwxrwxr-x    6 root       sys            512 Jan 26 17:37 home
lrwxrwxrwx    1 bin        bin              8 Oct 16  1990 lib -> /usr/lib
-rw-r--r--    1 root       sys              0 Oct 16  1990 quotas
drwxrwxrwt    2 sys        sys            512 Jun  7 08:40 tmp
lrwxrwxrwx    1 root       root            11 Jan 25 13:17 unix -> /stand/unix
drwxrwxr-x   19 root       sys            512 Jan 25 13:09 usr
drwxrwxr-x   16 root       sys            512 Jun  7 08:24 var
$ _
```

This example output is a subset of the complete long listing for the root directory listed previously. The long listing format provides a great deal of information about the files referred to by the directory's entries. From left to right, the columns in this format are defined as follows:

• Mode – the file mode consisting of the file's type and access permissions. This field will be explained in more detail in Section 2.7.9.

• Links – the number of (hard) links to the file.

• Owner – the login name of the file's owner.

• Group – the group name of the file's group.

• Size – the size of the file in bytes.

• Month – the month when the file was last modified.

- Day – the day when the file was last modified.

- Time/year – the time when the file was last modified. However, if the file was not modified within the current year, this field contains the year when the file was last modified.

- File name – the file name portion of the directory entry. If the directory entry is a soft link, this field also contains the pathname to which the link refers.

The mode field breaks down into four fields as follows:

1. File type, 1 character. This character may take any of the following values:

   d The file is a directory.

   b The file is a block special file, that is, a block I/O device.

   c The file is a character special file, that is, a character I/O device. Terminal devices are typical character devices.

   p The file is a named pipe.

   l The directory entry is a soft link.

   – The file is an ordinary file.

2. Owner permissions, three characters. This field indicates the access permissions applicable to the file's owner. The three characters represent, in order from left to right, *read*, *write*, and *execute* permissions. rwx depicts the case when read, write, and execute access are all permitted. A hyphen (-) in any position means that the respective access right is denied. For example, r-x indicates that read and execute access are permitted, write access is denied. If the field contains all hyphens, that is, the field appears ---, all access is denied.

3. Group permissions, three characters. This field indicates the access permissions applicable to the file's group.

4. other (or public) permissions, three characters - this field indicates the access permissions applicable to all users other than the file's owner and members of the file's group.

It is common to use **ls** to list information about a directory instead of its contents. Suppose you wished to learn the status of the /usr/bin directory and issued the following command:

```
$ ls -l /usr/bin<CR>
total 12086
-r-xr-xr-x    2 bin       bin        52172 Oct 15   1990 STTY
-rwxr-xr-x    1 bin       bin        22736 Oct 15   1990 acctcom
-r-xr-xr-x    1 bin       bin        45848 Oct 15   1990 ar
  .
  .
  .
-r-xr-xr-x    1 bin       bin         6464 Oct  1   1990 ypcat
-r-xr-xr-x    1 bin       bin         6040 Oct  1   1990 ypmatch
-r-xr-xr-x    1 bin       bin         8016 Oct  1   1990 ypwhich
-r-xr-xr-x    3 bin       bin        10584 Oct 15   1990 zcat
$ _
```

ls dutifully produces a long listing of the /usr/bin directory's contents instead of a listing on the directory itself. This works correctly if the argument to **ls** is a file. For example:

```
$ ls -l /usr/bin/ls<CR>
-r-xr-xr-x    2 bin       bin        12308 Oct 15   1990 /usr/bin/ls
$ _
```

However, when the argument to **ls** is a directory, **ls** lists information regarding the directory's contents, not the directory itself. The -d option causes **ls** to list information about a directory instead of its contents:

```
$ ls -ld /usr/bin<CR>
drwxrwxr-x    2 bin       bin         5120 Jan 25 13:15 /usr/bin
$ _
```

Here you can see the mode, owner, size, and so on, for the /usr/bin directory.

2.7.2   cat - Concatenate and Print Files

cat was introduced earlier in the chapter. One of its two options is -s, which causes **cat** to remain silent about nonexistent files. For example:

```
$ cat /etc/passwd /etc/password<CR>
root:x:0:1:0000-Admin(0000):/:
daemon:x:1:1:0000-Admin(0000):/:
    .
    .
    .
robm:x:1000:1:Robert Martin:/home/robm:
pal:x:1001:1:Phil Laplante:/home/pal:
cat: cannot open /etc/password
$ _
```

cat complains that it cannot open the file **/etc/password**. This is fine if the user is interested. However, there are cases where the user is interested only in what exists and doesn't care about non-existent files. Therefore:

```
$ cat -s /etc/passwd /etc/password<CR>
root:x:0:1:0000-Admin(0000):/:
daemon:x:1:1:0000-Admin(0000):/:
bin:x:2:2:0000-Admin(0000):/usr/bin:
    .
    .
    .
robm:x:1000:1:Robert Martin:/home/robm:
pal:x:1001:1:Phil Laplante:/home/pal:
$ _
```

suppresses the complaint about the non-existant **/etc/password**.

2.7.3   tail - Print Tail Portion of File

tail is similar to **cat** in that it prints files to standard output. However, **tail** allows the user to be a bit more selective. **tail** starts its output from a user-specified point within the file and continues until it reaches the end of the file. By default, it starts its output 10 lines from the end of the file:

```
$ tail /etc/passwd<CR>
adm:x:4:4:0000-Admin(0000):/var/adm:
uucp:x:5:5:0000-uucp(0000):/usr/lib/uucp:
lp:x:7:8:0000-LP(0000):/home/lp:/sbin/sh
service:x:9:9:Service Login:/service:
nuucp:x:10:10:0000-uucp(0000):/var/spool/uucppublic:/usr/lib/uucp/uucico
listen:x:37:4:Network Admin:/usr/net/nls:
sync:x:67:1:0000-Admin(0000):/:/usr/bin/sync
install:x:101:1:Initial Login:/home/install:
robm:x:1000:1:Robert Martin:/home/robm:
pal:x:1001:1:Phil Laplante:/home/pal:
$ _
```

In this example, **tail** printed the last 10 lines of the password file.

The starting offset can be modified so that additional or fewer lines are included in the output:

```
$ tail -5 /etc/passwd<CR>
listen:x:37:4:Network Admin:/usr/net/nls:
sync:x:67:1:0000-Admin(0000):/:/usr/bin/sync
install:x:101:1:Initial Login:/home/install:
robm:x:1000:1:Robert Martin:/home/robm:
pal:x:1001:1:Phil Laplante:/home/pal:
$ _
```

The option $-n$, where n is an integer value, specifies the starting offset from the end of the file. **tail** can also be instructed to key on characters or blocks instead of lines. For example, to print the last 10 characters of a file:

```
$ tail -c /etc/passwd<CR>
home/pal:
$ _
```

The -c option instructs **tail** to measure files in characters instead of lines. The -b option calls for **tail** to measure files in blocks.

Replacing the hyphen with a plus sign instructs **tail** to start output relative to the top of the file rather than the end of the file. For example, an argument value of +8 causes **tail** to start its output at the eighth line, that is, to print the entire file except for the first seven lines:

```
$ tail +8 /etc/passwd<CR>
service:x:9:9:Service Login:/service:
nuucp:x:10:10:0000-uucp(0000):/var/spool/uucppublic:/usr/lib/uucp/uu
listen:x:37:4:Network Admin:/usr/net/nls:
sync:x:67:1:0000-Admin(0000):/:/usr/bin/sync
install:x:101:1:Initial Login:/home/install:
robm:x:1000:1:Robert Martin:/home/robm:
pal:x:1001:1:Phil Laplante:/home/pal:
$ _
```

Perhaps the most useful option is **-f**. Given this option, **tail** does not exit when it reaches the end of the file. Instead, it continues to read the file periodically and outputs additional lines as they are appended. **tail** continues to wait for and print additional lines until the user halts the program. This feature, which can't be adequately demonstrated here since its output appears over time, is especially useful for monitoring logs.

2.7.4 cp - Copy Files

cp copies files and directories. In simplest form:

cp *srcfile destfile*

makes a copy of the file *srcfile* called *destfile*, where *srcfile* and *destfile* can be simple file names or pathnames. If the destination file does not exist, **cp** creates it. Otherwise, **cp** overwrites it with the contents of *srcfile*. For example:

```
$ cp /etc/group /tmp/group<CR>
$ _
```

creates a copy of the group file in the **/tmp** directory. The following command replaces the contents of /tmp/group with the contents of the password file:

```
$ cp /etc/passwd /tmp/group<CR>
$ _
```

The destination file name remains unchanged. However, its contents are replaced with that of **/etc/passwd**.

Frequently, it is necessary or desirable to copy more than one file at a time. This is accomplished with the following syntax:

cp *srcfile1* [*srcfile2...*] *destdir*

where *srcfile1*, *srcfile2*, through *srcfileN* are ordinary files and *destdir* is a directory. **cp** creates a copy of each source file in the destination directory. Within the destination directory, an existing file with the same name as one of the source files is overwritten—new files are created as needed. The first example in this section could have been accomplished with this syntax as follows:

```
$ cp /etc/group /tmp<CR>
$ _
```

The result is the same. A copy of the group file is placed in the /tmp directory. A more typical example is:

```
$ cp module1.c module2.c module3.c /home/robm/tmp<CR>
$ ls /home/robm/tmp<CR>
module1.c
module2.c
module3.c
$ _
```

Three files are copied from the current directory into the directory /home/robm/tmp. Of course, it could have been done more efficiently as follows:

```
$ cp *[0-9].c /home/robm/tmp<CR>
$ _
```

The shell expands *[0-9].c into the list module1.c module2.c module3.c and passes the list as arguments to **cp**. Copying multiple files in this fashion, that is, with a single **cp** command, is allowed only when the destination file is a directory.

Instead of listing each file explicitly or using a file name pattern, an entire directory may be copied using the following syntax:

cp -r *srcdir destdir*

Both *srcdir* and *destdir* must be directories. **cp** replicates the source directory and all of its descendants in the target directory. Consider the following examples:

```
$ cp /home/pal /tmp<CR>
cp: </home/pal> directory
$ cp -r /home/pal /tmp<CR>
$ ls -ld /tmp/pal
drwxrwxr-x   2 robm      other          512 Jun 25 11:43 /tmp/pal
$ ls -la /tmp/pal
total 6
drwxrwxr-x   2 robm      other          512 Jun 25 11:43 .
drwxrwxrwt   4 sys       sys            512 Jun 25 11:43 ..
-rw-r--r--   1 robm      other          472 Jun 25 11:43 .profile
$ _
```

Without the -r option, **cp** will not copy a directory. With the -r option, **cp** created /tmp/pal and copied the descendants of /home/pal into it. In this case, there are no descendants and only one file—.profile. This example was chosen to illustrate the point and it is harmless enough. However, copying a directory that has numerous descendants may consume a large amount of file space. Furthermore, copying a directory into one of its descendants creates a recursive copy operation that will consume all available disk space. Exercise great care when copying directories.

cp is another example of the characteristic silence of Unix commands. All too often, this silence may lead to unfortunate results. Unix commands tend to be silent due to the frequent use of command pipelines and I/O redirection where extraneous text is undesirable. However, the drawback, especially in this case, is that sometimes the user doesn't receive potentially useful information. With **cp**, the user has no idea whether **cp** is destroying existing files unless he or she explicitly asks for this information. The -i option prevents **cp** from silently carrying out destructive copies:

```
$ cp -i /etc/passwd /tmp/group<CR>
cp: overwrite /tmp/group? n<CR>
$ _
```

When -i is specified, **cp** prompts the user regarding any existing destination files that might be overwritten and thus destroyed. The user responds with **y** to overwrite the file or **n** to leave the file untouched.

2.7.5 mv - Move Files

The **mv** command is similar to **cp** except that it moves files and directories instead of copying them. Its simplest form is:

mv *srcfile destfile*

which moves *srcfile* to *destfile*. Unlike **cp** however, *srcfile* ceases to exist as a result of the move.

If the source and destination files appear in the same directory, moving a file amounts to changing its name:

```
$ ls mod*.c<CR>
module1.c
$ mv module1.c module4.c<CR>
$ ls mod*.c<CR>
module4.c
$ _
```

Multiple files are moved with the following syntax:

mv *srcfile1* [*srcfile2...*] *destdir*

The source files *srcfile1*, *srcfile2*, through *srcfileN* are moved from their current directory to the destination directory *destdir*.

Like **cp**, **mv** can be destructive. When an existing file has the same name as the destination file or appears in the destination directory and matches the name of one of the source files, it is removed and replaced with the contents of the source file. Consider the following:

```
$ ls /tmp/*.c<CR>
/tmp/module4.c
$ mv module2.c /tmp/module4.c<CR>
$ mv -i module3.c /tmp/module4.c<CR>
mv: overwrite /tmp/module4.c? n<CR>
$ _
```

In the first example, /tmp/module4.c is silently replaced with module2.c. In the second example, -i caused **mv** to report the existence of the destination file and prompt the user for direction. If the user responds with y, the destination file is replaced. Otherwise, it remains intact and the move does not take place.

Ordinary and special files can be moved from one file system to another. Directories may be moved only within a file system. Suppose that /home and /tmp appear on separate file systems. Consider the following:

```
$ ls /home/robm/code/*.c<CR>
/home/robm/code/module1.c
/home/robm/code/module2.c
/home/robm/code/module3.c
/home/robm/code/module4.c
$ mv /home/robm/code /tmp<CR>
mv: can't mv directories across file systems
$ mv /home/robm/code /home/robm/c_code<CR>
$ mv /home/robm/c_code/*.c /tmp<CR>
$ ls /tmp/*.c<CR>
/tmp/module1.c
/tmp/module2.c
/tmp/module3.c
/tmp/module4.c
$ ls /home/robm/c_code/*.c
/home/robm/c_code/*.c: No such file or directory
$ _
```

The directory /home/robm/code cannot be moved to /tmp since /tmp and /home reside on separate file systems. /home/robm/code is moved (renamed) to /home/robm/c_code because the move occurs within a file system. Finally, the source code files are moved individually to /tmp.

2.7.6   rm - Remove Files

The **rm** command removes files. The basic syntax for **rm** is:

rm *file1* [*file2...*]

where *file1*, *file2*, through *fileN* is a list of files to be removed. For each file name in the argument list, **rm** removes the associated directory entry. If the deleted entry was the only remaining hard link to the file, the file itself is removed.

As with both **cp** and **mv**, **rm** can be very destructive. The -i option, demonstrated in the following example, prevents the accidental loss of files:

```
$ rm -i *.c<CR>
rm: remove   module1.c: (y/n)? n
rm: remove   module2.c: (y/n)? n
rm: remove   module3.c: (y/n)? n
rm: remove   module4.c: (y/n)? n
$ _
```

With this option, the user is prompted for a y or n response for each file in the argument list. This is especially useful when using file name patterns to delete files. **rm** automatically prompts the user in a similar fashion for each file in the argument list that the user owns but is denied write permission. For example:

```
$ ls -l /tmp/module1.c<CR>
-r--r--r--    1 robm      other            0 Jun 25 14:34 /tmp/module1.c
$ rm /tmp/module1.c<CR>
rm: /tmp/module1.c: 444 mode ? n
$ _
```

There are occasions where a directory and all of its descendants need to be deleted. For this purpose, the -r option causes **rm** to remove each directory that appears in the argument list, along with all of their files and descendants.

```
$ ls /home/robm/c_code<CR>
module1.c
module2.c
module3.c
module4.c
$ rm -r /home/robm/c_code<CR>
$ ls /home/robm/c_code<CR>
/home/robm/c_code: No such file or directory
$ _
```

With one command, the directory, its files, and all of its descendants are removed from the system. Exercise the utmost care when using this command!

2.7.7   file - Identify File Type

The **file** command is useful for determining the nature of a file without using **cat** or **pg**. **file** offers an explanation for each file in its argument list:

```
$ file /home/robm /home/robm/.profile /usr/bin/file /usr/bin/clear<CR>
/home/robm: directory
/home/robm/.profile: ascii text
/usr/bin/file: ELF 32-bit LSB executable 80386 Version 1
/usr/bin/clear: commands text
```

In this example, **file** reports that

- /home/robm is a directory.

- /home/robm/.profile is an ASCII text file.

- /usr/bin/file is a binary executable program file.

- /usr/bin/clear is a commands text or shell script file.

Unfortunately, **file** isn't perfect. It reports /home/robm/.profile is an ASCII file when in fact it is also a commands text file. However, since .profile is an ASCII file, it can be examined further with **cat** or **pg**.

2.7.8   type - Identify Command Type

The **type** command is similar to **file** in that it reports the nature of user commands. For example:

```
$ type echo ls<CR>
echo is a shell builtin
ls is /usr/bin/ls
$ _
```

type reports the full pathname of an external command's program file (for example, **ls**) and shell builtin for the shell's internal commands (for example, **echo**). This command is especially useful if there are multiple versions of a particular command on a system.

2.7.9   chmod - Change File Mode

The **chmod** command changes the access mode for files and directories. Its basic syntax is:

chmod *mode file1* [*file2...*]

where *mode* specifies the desired access mode and *file1*, *file2*, through *fileN* is a list of files and directories.

The *mode* value can be specified numerically or symbolically. Numerically, an access mode specification is a three-digit octal number. The first digit represents the owner's permissions, the second represents the group's permissions, and the third represents the permissions granted to all other users. Discrete values represent read, write, and execute permission; a value of 4 indicates the read access is allowed, 2 indicates that write access is allowed, and 1 indicates that execute access is allowed. The permissions granted to a particular user class is the sum of the individual read, write, and execute values assigned to that user class. A 0 indicates that all permissions are denied. For example:

000 All access denied.

100 Execute by owner is allowed.

200 Write by owner is allowed.

300 Write and execute by owner is allowed.

400 Read by owner is allowed.

500 Read and execute by owner is allowed.

600 Read and write by owner is allowed.

700 read, write, and execute by owner are allowed.

070 read, write, and execute by group are allowed.

007 read, write, and execute by other allowed.

777 read, write, and execute by owner, group, and other are allowed.

To change the mode of a file to read only for all users:

```
$ chmod 444 /tmp/group<CR>
$ ls -l /tmp/group<CR>
-r--r--r--   1 robm      other          572 Jun 25 12:32 /tmp/group
$ _
```

To change the mode of a file such that all users can read and execute the file but only the owner can write to the file:

```
$ chmod 755 command<CR>
$ ls -l command<CR>
-rwxr-xr-x   1 robm      other          572 Jun 25 12:32 command
$ _
```

In symbolic form, `mode` is expressed as follows:

user_group operation permissions

where *user_group* represents one or more of the owner, group, and other user groups, *operation* indicates whether permission is enabled, disabled, or assigned, and *permissions* represents the access permissions. User classes are represented as follows:

u represents the file's owner.

g represents the file's group.

o represents all users other than the file's owner and group.

Operations are defined as follows:

= assigns permissions.

+ grants permission.

- denies permission.

Permissions are represented by the characters used in a long listing:

r represents read access.

w represents write access.

x represents execute access.

They are used, for example, to assign the owner read, write, and execute permission:

chmod o=rwx *filename*

To add execute permission for the file's group and remove write permission from all users except the file's owner and group:

chmod g+x,o-w *filename*

2.8   Directory Commands

This section describes commands devoted exclusively to the use and management of directories.

2.8.1   cd - Change Directory

cd is perhaps the simplest of Unix commands and certainly one of the most frequently used. Its syntax is:

cd [*directory*]

If *directory* is not specified, the user's home directory becomes the current directory. Otherwise *directory* becomes the current directory. For example:

```
$ cd /tmp<CR>
$ pwd<CR>
/tmp
$ cd<CR>
$ pwd<CR>
/home/robm
$ _
```

A file name pattern may be used to specify a directory. However, if the pattern expands into multiple directories, the first directory in the list becomes the current directory. Finally, if the specified directory doesn't exist:

```
$ cd /tmp/nodir<CR>
/tmp/nodir: does not exist
$ _
```

2.8.2   mkdir - Make Directory

mkdir creates directories. Its basic syntax is:

```
mkdir newdir
```

where *newdir* is the directory to be created. If the target directory is specified without a pathname, it is created in the current directory; that is:

```
mkdir newdir
```

is equivalent to the command

```
mkdir ./newdir
```

If a full or relative pathname is specified, the target directory is created in the appropriate place in the hierarchy. For example:

```
$ mkdir /tmp/newdir<CR>
$ ls -ld /tmp/newdir<CR>
drwxr-xr-x   2 robm      other        512 Jun 25 20:17 /tmp/newdir
$ _
```

However, each directory appearing in the pathname except for the target directory, that is, each directory except the one terminating the pathname, must exist. If not, **mkdir** complains:

```
$ mkdir /tmp/newdir1/newdir2/lastdir<CR>
mkdir:  Failed to make directory "/tmp/newdir1/newdir2/lastdir";
No such file or directory
$ _
```

The -p option instructs **mkdir** to create any directory that appears in the pathname as needed:

```
$ mkdir -p /tmp/newdir1/newdir2/lastdir<CR>
$ ls -ld /tmp/newdir1/newdir2/lastdir<CR>
drwxr-xr-x   2 robm   other     512 Jun 25 20:37 /tmp/newdir1/newdir2/lastdir
$ _
```

The default access mode for new directories is 777. However, the default access mode is altered according to the *umask* value. The umask value is subtracted from the default access mode to produce a new value for creating directories. A typical value for umask is 022. Subtracting 022 from 777 yields 755. A directory created with 755 access mode has permissions of:

```
drwxr-xr-x
```

All permissions are granted to the owner, read/execute permissions are granted to file's group, and read/execute permissions are granted to all other users. To learn what the umask value is, simply type **umask** as follows:

```
$ umask<CR>
022
$ _
```

The **umask** value is set as follows:

```
$ umask 022<CR>
$ _
```

2.8.3   rmdir - Remove Directory

rmdir removes directories. Its syntax is similar to that of **rm**:

rmdir *dirname1* [*dirname2...*]

Each empty directory in the argument list is removed. For example:

```
$ rmdir /tmp/newdir<CR>
$ ls -ld /tmp/newdir<CR>
/tmp/newdir: No such file or directory
$ _
```

Attempting to remove a non-empty directory produces the following error message:

```
$ rmdir /tmp/newdir1<CR>
rmdir: /tmp/newdir1: Directory not empty
$ _
```

Recall from the discussion of **rm** that non-empty directories can be removed as follows:

```
$ rm -r /tmp/newdir1<CR>
$ ls -ld /tmp/newdir1<CR>
/tmp/newdir1: No such file or directory
$ _
```

2.9 Additional Shell Features

This section contains an introduction to some of the shell's more advanced features.

2.9.1 Multiple Commands on a Line

Commands are usually typed one to a line. Two or more commands can be typed on a single line if they are separated by a semi-colon character (;):

```
$ cd /; pwd; ls -CF; cd; pwd<CR>
/
altboot*     etc/        install/      opt/        service/     u/
bin@         export/     lib@          proc/       shlib/       unix@
dev/         home/       lost+found/   quotas      stand/       usr/
dgn*         home2/      mnt/          sbin/       tmp/         var/
/home/robm
$ _
```

Each command is processed sequentially as if it had been typed on a separate line. However, none of the commands is executed until a carriage return is typed.

2.9.2   Command Substitution

When parsing a command line, the shell interprets any string enclosed in accent graves (') as a command. It executes the command and replaces the string with the resulting output. This is somewhat analogous to the expansion of file name patterns. The shell replaces a file name pattern with a list of files. Similarly, it replaces a string enclosed in accent graves with the command's output.

Consider the following:

```
$ cd /; echo *<CR>
altboot bin dev dgn etc export home home2 install lib lost+found mnt
opt proc quotas sbin service shlib stand tmp u unix usr var

$ echo 'ls /'
altboot bin dev dgn etc export home home2 install lib lost+found mnt
opt proc quotas sbin service shlib stand tmp u unix usr var
```

These commands produced the same result using different methods. In the first example, the user changed to the root directory and listed all files matching the file name pattern *, that is, the contents of the root directory. The listing in the second example was produced by the imbedded **ls** command.

2.9.3   I/O Redirection

The shell allows the user to redirect a command's standard input, standard output, and standard error I/O streams.

The shell interprets a string preceded by a greater-than character (>) as the name (or pathname) of an ordinary or special file and directs the command's standard output into that file or device. For instance, the command:

```
cat /etc/passwd > /tmp/passwd
```

is similar to:

```
cp /etc/passwd /tmp/passwd
```

The output of the **cat** command, in this case the contents of the password file, is directed to the ordinary file **/tmp/passwd**. **/tmp/passwd** is created if it doesn't exist. Otherwise, its contents is replaced. However, **cp** replicates the permissions of the source file—**cat** creates a new file with the default permissions.

Output is appended to a file as follows:

```
cat /etc/passwd >> /tmp/passwd
```

The target file, similar to the previous version, is created if it does not exist. However, if the file exists, the command's output is appended to the file instead of replacing it.

Standard error output is redirected by preceding > or >> with 2. Consider this variation on an example from Section 2.7.2:

```
$ cat /etc/passwd /etc/password 2> /tmp/stderr.out<CR>
root:x:0:1:0000-Admin(0000):/:
daemon:x:1:1:0000-Admin(0000):/:
bin:x:2:2:0000-Admin(0000):/usr/bin:
 .

 .

 .

robm:x:1000:1:Robert Martin:/home/robm:
pal:x:1001:1:Phil Laplante:/home/pal:
$ _
```

The error message about **/etc/password** seems to be missing. However, since **cat** outputs error messages to standard error instead of standard output, the missing message is contained in **/tmp/stderr.out**:

```
$ cat /tmp/stderr.out<CR>
cat: cannot open /etc/password
$ _
```

The shell interprets a string preceded by a less-than character (<) as the name (or pathname) of an ordinary or special file and reads the command's input from that file or device. Mailing a lengthy message to another user is a typical use of input redirection. The message is usually prepared by an editor, stored in a text file, and sent to the user as follows:

```
mail user < mesgfile
```

A period in the first column of the file's last line is not needed—**mail** recognizes the end of the file without it.

2.9.4 Pipelines

Pipelines take advantage of both I/O redirection and the modular nature of Unix commands to create complex processes. A pipeline is two or more Unix commands separated by the pipe character (|):

command1 | *command2* | *command3* ...

command1's output is redirected to the input of *command2*, which in turn is redirected to the input of *command3*, and so on. For instance, lengthy directory listings are easily managed by piping **ls**'s output to **pg**:

```
$ ls -l /usr/bin | pg -5<CR>
total 11986
-r-xr-xr-x   2 bin      bin          52172 Oct 15   1990 STTY
-rwxr-xr-x   1 bin      bin          22736 Oct 15   1990 acctcom
-r-xr-xr-x   1 bin      bin          45848 Oct 15   1990 ar
-r-sr-xr-x   1 root     sys          29128 Oct 15   1990 at
:<CR>
-r-sr-xr-x   1 root     sys          13684 Oct 15   1990 atq
-r-sr-xr-x   1 root     sys          12244 Oct 15   1990 atrm
-r-xr-xr-x   2 bin      bin          56076 Oct 15   1990 awk
lrwxrwxrwx   1 root     root            16 Oct 16   1990 backup -> /usr/bin/.bac
:q<CR>
```

2.9.5   Background Processing

Most commands are run in the *foreground*. The shell invokes a child process to carry out a user's command and waits for it to complete before to accepting another command. *Background processing* allows a user to run commands in such a way that the shell immediately accepts his or her next command without waiting for the child process to exit. This is commonly used when compiling programs—the compiler is run in the background, its output is redirected to a log file, and the programmer monitors its progress with the **ps** command and the log.

The syntax to run a command in the background is:

```
$ command &<CR>
PID
$ _
```

where **command** is any Unix command line and **PID** is the process ID of the resulting child process.

The **kill** command halts a background process prematurely:

```
kill pid
```

where *pid* is a PID reported by the shell when the background process was started. **kill** sends the process a signal that usually causes it to terminate. On occasion, the process ignores the default signal and continues to run. In such cases, the user can forcibly terminate the process with:

```
kill -9 pid
```

The -9 option sends a signal that cannot be ignored. This signal is sometimes called "the teflon bullet."

Normally, if a user logs out with a process running in the background, the process is halted. **nohup**, for "no hangup," allows a user to start a command in the background and leave it running even after he or she logs out:

```
nohup command & <CR>
pid
$ _
```

where *command* is a user command and *pid* is the process ID of the process running that command.

A cautionary note regarding background processes—an interactive command, that is, a command that receives input from or writes output to the user, should not be run in the background. It can cause unpredictable results and is difficult to correct.

2.9.6 Escaping and Quoting Special Characters

Occasionally it is necessary or desirable to use a character that has special meaning to the shell as an ordinary character. An example of this was demonstrated in the section describing the **stty** command.

A backslash character (\) preceding a special character causes the shell to treat it as an ordinary character:

```
$ echo mod\*.c<CR>
mod*.c

$ echo \'hello world\'<CR>
'hello world'

$ _
```

In the first example, file name expansion did not occur because the asterisk was treated literally. In the second example, command substitution was suppressed. Note that both accent graves were escaped. If a single accent grave was escaped, the shell would continue the command on additional lines until the matching accent grave was typed:

```
$ echo \'hello world'<CR>
> <CR>
> <CR>
> '<CR>
'hello world
$ _
```

> is the secondary shell prompt. This prompt is displayed on a new line when a user types an incomplete command and presses the carriage return. Even the carriage return can be escaped:

```
$ ls \<CR>
> -l \<CR>
> /usr/bin | \<CR>
> pg -5<CR>
total 11986
-r-xr-xr-x   2 bin      bin       52172 Oct 15   1990 STTY
-rwxr-xr-x   1 bin      bin       22736 Oct 15   1990 acctcom
-r-xr-xr-x   1 bin      bin       45848 Oct 15   1990 ar
-r-sr-xr-x   1 root     sys       29128 Oct 15   1990 at
: q<CR>
$ _
```

This is occasionally useful when typing a long command.

All characters enclosed within double quotes (") are treated as ordinary characters except for the dollar sign ($), accent graves ('), and the backslash (\):

```
$ echo "*"<CR>
*

$ echo "`pwd`"<CR>
/home/robm

$ echo "\`pwd\`"
`pwd`

$ echo "$PATH"<CR>
/usr/bin:/usr/ucb
$ _
```

Command and shell variable substitution still take place within double quotes—file name generation does not.

All characters enclosed within single quotes (') are treated as ordinary characters except for the dollar sign ($) and the single quote itself:

```
$ echo '*'<CR>
*

$ echo '`pwd`'<CR>
`pwd`

$ echo '\`pwd\`'
\`pwd\`

$ echo '$PATH'
/usr/bin:/usr/ucb
$ _
```

Whitespace, the default field separator, must also be quoted to create a string containing whitespace:

```
$ USER=Rob Martin<CR>
Martin: not found

$ USER="Rob Martin"<CR>
$ echo $USER<CR>
Rob Martin
$ _
```

The shell permits variable assignment statements preceding any command. In the first example, the shell treated USER=Rob as a variable assignment and

attempted to execute `Martin` as a command. The second example correctly
quotes the space character to produce the complete string `Rob Martin`,
which is then assigned to the variable `USER`.

2.10   Additional Commands

This section contains an introduction to additional commands including
some frequently used filters. In general, these commands are more advanced
than those described previously.

2.10.1   which - Which Command

which is similar to **type** in that it reports the pathnames of user
commands:

```
$ which ls type<CR>
/usr/bin/ls
no type in /usr/bin /usr/ucb
```

Unlike **type**, **which** cannot detect internal shell commands. It reports that
these commands are not found in any of the directories listed in the `PATH`
variable.

2.10.2   lp - Line Printer

lp submits print jobs to the print spooler. The simplest form of **lp** is:

```
$ lp filename<CR>
request-id is rid
$ _
```

where *filename* is the name or pathname of the file to be printed and *rid* is
an identifier assigned to the print job. If *filename* is not present, **lp** prints
its standard input, A frequently used syntax is:

```
cat filename | lp
```

Without additional options or arguments, a print job is spooled to the system's default printer. A specific printer is specified with the −d option as follows:

```
$ lp -d prname filename<CR>
request-id is rid
$ _
```

where *prname* is the name, that is, symbolic address, of one of the system's printers.

The −m option causes the print spooler to send mail to a print job's originator when the job is finished:

```
$ lp -d prname -m filename<CR>
request-id is rid
$ _
```

Printer facilities vary greatly from installation to installation—in particular, the type and number of available printers as well as their symbolic addresses. Different print spooler packages are also employed at some installations. These commands may or may not work at your site. See your system administrator regarding local printers and submitting print jobs.

2.10.3 pr - Format and Print File

pr is an example of a *filter*, a command that transforms its standard input and prints the result to its standard output. Its simplest form is:

```
pr filename
```

where *filename* is the name or pathname of the file to be printed. Without arguments, **pr** formats the file into pages of 66 lines each. 10 lines are used for a page header and footer. The header consists of 2 blank lines, a line of text, and 2 blank lines. The default header text is the date and time, the file's name, and the page number. The default footer consists of 5 blank lines.

pr has a variety of options that alter the output format:

+*N* Start output at the *Nth* page.

-d Double space the output lines.

-n Number the output lines. This option is commonly used when print-ing source code.

-w*W* Set the page width, by default 72 columns, to *W* columns.

-l*L* Set the page length, by default 66 lines, to *L* lines.

-h *header* Replace the default header with the string *header*. A space is required between -h and *header*.

-f Separate pages with form feed characters instead of blank lines.

pr and **lp** are frequently combined in a pipeline similar to the following:

```
pr -n srcfile | lp
```

This pipeline formats and prints *srcfile*, including line numbers, on the system's default printer.

2.10.4   wc - Word Count

wc is another filter example that outputs, in order, the count of lines, words, and characters contained in an ordinary file. Its syntax is:

```
wc [-lwc] [filename...]
```

where *filename* is the name or pathname of the target file. If *filename* is not present, **wc** reads its standard input. If more than one *filename* is specified, **wc** prints a report for each file in the list preceded by its filename. The options cause **wc** to restrict its output to the count of lines, words, or characters respectively. For example, to count the lines in the password file:

```
$ cat /etc/passwd | wc -l<CR>
      14
$ _
```

2.10.5   ln - Link Files

ln creates directory entries, that is, links, including both hard and soft
links:

ln [-s] *target newlink*

where *newlink* is a new directory entry that will refer to the target file
target.
    By default, **ln** creates hard links:

```
$ ls -li /tmp/mod*.c<CR>
 3800 -rw-r--r--  1 robm     other         492 Jul  6 21:29 /tmp/module1.c

$ ln /tmp/module1.c /tmp/module2.c<CR>

$ ls -li /tmp/mod*.c<CR>
 3800 -rw-r--r--  2 robm     other         492 Jul  6 21:29 /tmp/module1.c
 3800 -rw-r--r--  2 robm     other         492 Jul  6 21:29 /tmp/module2.c
$ _
```

The initial **ls** command lists information pertaining to /tmp/module1.c
including its inode number (-i option). A new link, named module2.c,
is created by the **ln** command and the subsequent listing shows that both
directory entries, module1.c and module2.c, refer to the same file—the
inode number and other information are identical. Note also that the link
count increased from 1 to 2.
    A user cannot create a hard link to a directory:

```
$ ln /home/robm /tmp/robm<CR>
ln: </home/robm> directory
```

Only soft links to a directory are permitted:

```
$ ln -s /home/robm /tmp/robm<CR>
$ ls -l /tmp/robm<CR>
lrwxrwxrwx  1 robm     other          10 Jul  6 21:14 /tmp/robm -> /home/robm
$ _
```

    A user can change directories via a soft link. However, the results may
be surprising:

```
$ cd /tmp/robm; pwd<CR>
/home/robm
$ _
```

Changing directory to /tmp/robm set the current directory to /home/robm. This occurred because /tmp/robm is a soft link and not a directory. The **cd** command followed the soft link to find the directory.

2.10.6   grep - Regular Expression Filter

The **grep** command scans a text file or files searching for lines that contain a user-specified sequence of text. Each line that contains the specified text is printed to standard output. For example:

```
$ grep robm /etc/passwd<CR>
robm:x:1001:1:Robert Martin:/home/robm:
$ _
```

grep read the password file /etc/passwd and printed each line that contained the string robm—in this case the password entry for Robert Martin. Since **grep** is a filter, this example could have been accomplished with a pipeline as follows:

```
$ cat /etc/passwd | grep robm<CR>
robm:x:1001:1:Robert Martin:/home/robm:
$ _
```

producing the same result.

grep is often used to scan a series of files to determine which file contains the specified text:

```
$ grep -l robm /etc/passwd /etc/group<CR>
/etc/passwd
```

In this example, **grep** searched two files, /etc/passwd and /etc/group, for the string robm. The -l option causes **grep** to print a list of the files that contain the specified string— in this example, /etc/passwd.

A regular expression is a string that **grep** interprets as a representation of an entire class of strings. Regular expressions are similar to file name patterns except that they apply to character strings in a text file instead of file names within a directory. For example, the period (.) represents any single character. The following command scans the password file for strings that start with 100, followed by any single character, followed by a colon:

```
$ grep '100.:' /etc/passwd<CR>
robm:x:1001:1:Robert Martin:/home/robm:
pal:x:1002:1:Phil Laplante:/home/pal:
cj:x:1003:1:Cj Martin:/home/cj:
```

The result is a list of users with user IDs ranging from 1000 to 1009. In this example, the regular-expression ('100.:') is enclosed in single quotes. The quotes are not part of the expression—they prevent the shell from interpreting special characters that may appear within the expression. Some of the regular expression characters are also used for file name patterns. Enclosing the regular expression in quotes prevents the shell from attempting to expand it into a list of file names.

Much of the utility of the **grep** command stems from its use of regular expressions. Regular expressions, described in additional detail in Section 3.12.4, provide the user with a flexible and powerful means of specifying text strings to be located within a text file. In addition to **grep**, regular expressions are used in a variety of Unix commands and programs, including **vi**, the visual editor, **sed**, the stream editor, and **awk**, a pattern matching and field processing program. Because a complete treatment of regular expressions is beyond the scope of this text, the reader is encouraged to explore regular expressions through the reference materials listed in the bibliography.

2.10.7   sort - Sort File

sort is another filter—it sorts its input and writes the result to standard output:

```
$ sort /etc/passwd<CR>
adm:x:4:4:0000-Admin(0000):/var/adm:
bin:x:2:2:0000-Admin(0000):/usr/bin:
daemon:x:1:1:0000-Admin(0000):/:
install:x:101:1:Initial Login:/home/install:
listen:x:37:4:Network Admin:/usr/net/nls:
lp:x:7:8:0000-LP(0000):/home/lp:/sbin/sh
nuucp:x:10:10:0000-uucp(0000):/var/spool/uucppublic:/usr/lib/uucp/uucico
pal:x:1001:1:Phil Laplante:/home/pal:
robm:x:1000:1:Robert Martin:/home/robm:
root:x:0:1:0000-Admin(0000):/:
service:x:9:9:Service Login:/service:
sync:x:67:1:0000-Admin(0000):/:/usr/bin/sync
sys:x:3:3:0000-Admin(0000):/:
uucp:x:5:5:0000-uucp(0000):/usr/lib/uucp:
```

As with most filters, **sort** reads its standard input if a file is not specified
on the command line:

```
$ cat /etc/passwd | sort<CR>
adm:x:4:4:0000-Admin(0000):/var/adm:
bin:x:2:2:0000-Admin(0000):/usr/bin:
daemon:x:1:1:0000-Admin(0000):/:

     .

     .

     .

sys:x:3:3:0000-Admin(0000):/:
uucp:x:5:5:0000-uucp(0000):/usr/lib/uucp:
```

By default, sorting occurs in ascending lexical order:

```
$ cat /tmp/alphas<CR>
c
b
a
C
B
A
```

```
$ sort /tmp/alphas<CR>
A
B
C
a
b
c
$ _
```

The -r option causes **sort** to reverse the default sorting order:

```
$ sort /tmp/alphas | sort -r<CR>
c
b
a
C
B
A
$ _
```

Unless otherwise specified, **sort** treats each line, in its entirety, as the sort key. However, a user may specify both a field separator and one or more key fields:

```
$ sort -t: +3 -4 -n -u /etc/passwd<CR>
daemon:x:1:1:0000-Admin(0000):/:
bin:x:2:2:0000-Admin(0000):/usr/bin:
sys:x:3:3:0000-Admin(0000):/:
listen:x:37:4:Network Admin:/usr/net/nls:
uucp:x:5:5:0000-uucp(0000):/usr/lib/uucp:
lp:x:7:8:0000-LP(0000):/home/lp:/sbin/sh
service:x:9:9:Service Login:/service:
nuucp:x:10:10:0000-uucp(0000):/var/spool/uucppublic:/usr/lib/uucp/uucico
$ _
```

This example includes a number of options:

-tc Causes **sort** to use the character c as the field separator, in this example the colon (:).

+$m.n$ Specifies the starting position of a sort key field—the $n+1st$ character of the $m+1st$ field. In this example, n assumes its default value of zero so the sort key starts at the *1st* character of the *4th* field.

-*m.n* Specifies the ending position of a sort key. This option is valid only
     when preceded by a +*m.n* option. The sort key ends at the *nth* char-
     acter following the *mth* field. In this example, the sort key ends at
     the *0th* character following the *4th* field.

  -n Numerically sorts keys which appear to be numeric values.

  -u Reduces the output to one line per unique sort key.

The result is one line from the `/etc/passwd` file for each unique key value
sorted numerically on the fourth field.

   If multiple files are specified, **sort** carries out a sort and merge operation.
Each file is sorted, and the results are merged together into a single output
stream.

2.10.8   find - Find File

find conducts a search of the directory hierarchy and executes a user specified action for each file that satisfies a user-specified criteria. Its syntax
is:

`find` *pathnamelist criteria action*

where *pathnamelist* is a list of one or more directories, *criteria* defines the
criteria for selecting files, and *action* is the action to be carried out.

   Various *criteria* expressions are used to select files from the hierarchy.
The most commonly used *criteria* is -**name**, as follows:

```
$ find / -name bin -print 2>/dev/null<CR>
/etc/conf/bin
/usr/lib/lp/bin
/usr/bin
/usr/alarm/bin
/usr/ccs/bin
/usr/sadm/bin
/usr/sadm/install/bin
/usr/sadm/sysadm/install/bin
/usr/sadm/sysadm/bin
/var/spool/lp/bin
/opt/bin
/bin
```

In this example, the pathname list consists of the root directory, the selection criteria is a file name of bin, and -print causes **find** to list each file that meets the criteria. Find searches every directory, to which the user has access in the hierarchy, and lists every file named bin. Error messages are redirected to /dev/null. /dev/null, also called the "bit bucket," is a special file that consumes all input and produces no output, that is, it is the system's trash can. **find** complains about directories it can't access so these messages were suppressed.

The power of **find** stems both from its ability to locate files in the hierarchy and to apply sophisticated actions with -exec:

```
$ find / -name bin -exec ls -id {} \; 2>/dev/null<CR>
 6248 /etc/conf/bin
17517 /usr/lib/lp/bin
 2688 /usr/bin
13440 /usr/alarm/bin
 4034 /usr/ccs/bin
 8078 /usr/sadm/bin
10787 /usr/sadm/install/bin
17484 /usr/sadm/sysadm/install/bin
   42 /usr/sadm/sysadm/bin
 4143 /var/spool/lp/bin
 2553 /opt/bin
  115 /bin
$ _
```

The string enclosed between -exec and an escaped semi-colon (\;) is treated as a shell command. This command is executed for each file that satisfies the criteria. Within the command, {} is replaced with the path-name of the current file. In this example, **find** prints the inode number for each of the **bin** directories contained in the hierarchy.

2.11 Exercises

1. Obtain your account information and log in to your system.

2. Change your password.

3. Attempt the examples presented in Section 2.3 and compare the results from your system with those presented in the text.

4. Obtain a list of the shell's variables and a list of the shell's environment. Explain the difference between the two.

5. The shell variable **$$** contains the PID of the shell process. Explain the outcome of

   ```
   cat /etc/passwd > /tmp/cat.$$
   ```

   Hint: keep in mind that the shell will fork a new process to execute the **cat** command.

6. Set the PATH variable to an emptry string and attempt a few commands including **echo**, **type**, **ls**, and **which**. Explain why each of the commands worked or failed. Restore the PATH variable to an appropriate value.

7. Create a shell variable called USERNAME containing your full name, including whitespace, and place it in the environment.

8. Use **stty** to disable echo of the erase character. Explain what happens when an erase character is typed and then restore erase character echo.

9. Set the erase character to a **t** and then set it back to <CTRL-h> (backspace).

10. Suppose that the current directory is empty and that the shell variable UNSETVAR does not exist. Explain the outcome of

    ```
    echo $UNSETVAR
    ```

and

```
echo *
```

11. Define an **echo** command that is equivalent to

```
ls -a
```

12. Define file name patterns to generate file names according to the following:

    (a) all files ending with a period (.) followed by any single character
    (b) All files ending with .c or .h
    (c) All starting with a lowercase character
    (d) All files starting with an alphabetic character
    (e) All files starting with anything other than a vowel

13. File name patterns should not be used to create directories. Explain. Hint: consider what happens if the pattern is expanded into a file list; if it is not expanded into a file list.

14. Define a **tail** command that is equivalent to

```
cat /etc/passwd
```

15. Suppose a file name pattern that expanded into a list of ordinary files was used as the destination of move command. Explain the outcome.

16. List the numeric and symbolic representation for the following access mode assignments:

    (a) Read/write for owner, read only for all other users
    (b) Read/write/execute for owner, read/execute for all other users
    (c) Read/write for owner, read only for group, all permissions denied for all other users
    (d) Execute only for all users
    (e) Read/write/execute for all users

17. Suppose a file's access mode is 000. Explain what the owner must do to read the file, write to the file, and to execute the file.

18. When a file is created, it is assigned an access mode in the same manner as a directory—the umask value is used to modify the default file access mode. Determine the default file access mode by creating a file, determining its access mode, and determining the current umask value.

19. Define the appropriate umask value to yield the following list of access modes for directories; for ordinary files.

    (a) 666

    (b) 444

    (c) 640

    (d) 711

20. Suppose the /tmp/robm is a soft link to /home/robm. Explain the outcome of:

    cd /tmp/robm; cd ..; pwd

21. Using command substitution and the **which** command, determine the file type of the **ls** and **which** commands. Explain why the **type** command cannot be substituted for **which**.

22. Explain the difference between the outcome of the following two commands:

    cat /etc/passwd /etc/group > /tmp/cat.out

    and

    cat /etc/passwd /etc/group >> /tmp/cat.out

23. For each of the following special characters, create a file with the character in its file name:

    (a) $

    (b) ?

    (c) <CTRL-h>

    (d) *

    (e) \

24. Using the appropriate commands, filters, and pipelines:

    (a) Obtain your own entry from the password file.

    (b) Obtain a count of users logged in to the system.

    (c) Obtain a sorted list of users logged in to the system.

    (d) Obtain a count of files in the /usr/bin directory.

25. Define a pipeline command that any of the system's users can use to print their login profile. The command must work without modification by the user. Assume that **lp** is the appropriate printer command.

26. Assume that the current directory contains a series of C language source code files. Define a command that will initiate an edit session for all of the source files that call the **printf** function.

27. The **find** command's criteria -**type d** selects directories. Using a pipeline, determine the number of accessible directories on the system.

Chapter 3

Using the Text Editor

This chapter discusses the standard and popular Unix System V full-screen editor, **vi** (for visual editor), and the basic concepts of creating and editing text files using this program. At the conclusion of this chapter, you will have acquired enough knowledge to create, modify, and maintain text files, in particular, C source code files.

3.1   Text File Structure and Basic Concepts

A source code file or other ASCII text file consists of a sequence of *lines* separated by *newline* characters. Newline characters are not visible, however, they are translated into "carriage return, line feed" sequences. On output each line of a text file appears on a separate line of the screen starting in the first column. A line consists of a sequence of *words*. A word is a sequence of alphanumeric characters terminated by *whitespace*, a punctuation mark, or some other non-alphanumeric character. Any string of adjacent punctuation marks or non-alphanumeric characters is also considered a word. Whitespace includes tab and space characters. Lines are implicitly numbered from 1 to n, where n is the number of lines in the file.

vi is not a word processor. It does not insert carriage returns, add pagination, indent paragraphs, provide margin justification, or perform many of the functions of a typical word processor. It is a text processor that allows the user to create, modify, and maintain ASCII text files. The user inserts tabs and carriage returns, and in all other respects determines the format of a file as it is edited. Lines whose length exceeds the right-hand margin are wrapped around to the next line on the display for the convenience of the user—this is a visual effect only.

As a file is edited, **vi** displays only the number of lines that will fit on the screen. For ASCII character terminals, this number is defined by the terminal type specified in the TERM environment variable. For windowing or graphical terminals, this number is defined by the window manager. In a sense, **vi** provides a screen-sized window into files much larger than the screen itself. **vi** loads files into an *edit buffer* and displays a portion of that buffer to the user. As a result, **vi** can edit very large files, although not arbitrarily large—some files are too large, and **vi** complains when such a file is loaded. The user can move the cursor and/or the window, add new text, modify existing text, delete text, and so forth. Changes do not take place to the file itself unless the user saves the edit buffer. The user can elect to save or abandon the edit buffer according to his or her needs and desires.

The current position within the buffer is marked by the *cursor*. On Unix systems, the cursor usually appears as a block or an underscore—

sometimes blinking, sometimes not. Within this text the cursor is depicted by an empty rectangle, a rectangle surrounding a character, or an underscore character (_). The lines displayed by **vi** are changed by moving the cursor or the window forward and backward. One or more tilde characters (~) indicate the end of the buffer. Tildes are visible when the window is positioned near the end of the buffer, so that the lines displayed cannot fill the screen or when the buffer is empty. An empty (new) file, depicted in Figure 3.1, appears as a screen full of tildes.

```




~
~
~
~
~
~
~
~
~
~
~
~
~
~
~
~
~
~
~
~
~
"filename" No such file or directory
```

Figure 3.1: The **vi** window into an empty file

3.2   Conventions Used in this Chapter

Throughout this chapter, discussions and examples are graphical where possible. A file and the *edit window* into a file is portrayed as in Figure 3.2. The empty rectangle represents the cursor position. The top of the file is sharp because it has a well-defined beginning. The end of the file is portrayed as ragged because the length of a file may vary as it is edited.

vi editing commands are illustrated with the following notation:

`filename`

`filename`

Figure 3.2: A file, the **vi** edit window, and the cursor position

old text with cursor . . .
+
user action
↓
new text with cursor . . .

where *old text* . . . represents one or more lines of existing text, *user action* depicts what the user types, and *new text* . . . is the resulting text. For example:

```
Peter Piper a peck ...
+
ipicked <ESC>
↓
Peter Piper picked_a peck ...
```

indicates that given the text

```
Peter Piper a peck ...
```

with the cursor positioned on the a and the user types

```
ipicked <ESC>
```

the resulting text is

```
Peter Piper picked_a peck ...
```

Note that this notation clearly depicts precisely what the user types and
its result on a given line of text.

3.3 Starting vi

vi is invoked as follows:

```
vi filename<CR>
```

where *filename* is the name of the file to be edited. **vi** loads the edit buffer with the file's contents, positions the edit window at the top of the file, and, after a short time, displays the edit window. If the file is too large for the edit buffer, **vi** issues an appropriate error message.

For example, suppose the file to be edited is named `hello.c` and it contains C language source code for a simple program. This file is edited as follows:

```
$ vi hello.c<CR>
```

Assuming `hello.c` exists in the current directory, the effect will look something like the following:

```
_
main()
{
        printf( "hello world\n" );
}
~
~

.

.

.
```

```
"hello.c" 5 lines 40 characters
```

If `hello.c` doesn't exist in the current directory, the display will look like Figure 3.1.

Prior to invoking **vi**, the terminal type variable `TERM` should be set appropriately and exported to the environment (see Chapter 2, Section 2.4.4).

3.4   Command Line Arguments to vi

vi accepts arguments other than the name of the file or files to be edited. One of these positions the cursor (and the edit window) at a line other than line 1. This is useful for editing large files when the line number is known. To use this feature, type:

```
vi +n filename<CR>
```

where *filename* is the name of the file to be edited and n is a line number where **vi** will position the cursor. The following command edits the example file `hello.c`, placing the cursor immediately on the 4th line, that is, on the `printf` statement:

```
$ vi +4 hello.c<CR>
```

The following variation on this form places the cursor at the end of the file:

```
vi + filename<CR>
```

3.5   Command Mode versus Edit Mode

vi operates in one of three modes—*command mode, edit mode*, and *extended command* mode. In command mode the user issues simple commands that perform operations such as moving the cursor or window and deleting a character or line. Many simple commands involve only a single keystroke, while others require two or more keystrokes. In edit mode each character typed by the user, except a backspace, `<CTRL-w>` and `<ESC>`, is inserted into the edit buffer. Depending on the command used to enter edit mode, the user may be adding new text or replacing existing text. The backspace character (in edit mode) erases the previous character. Successive backspace characters erase one character for each backspace typed until all characters on the current line have been erased. A `<CTRL-w>` erases the previous word, and `<ESC>` exits edit mode. Extended command mode gives the user access to advanced commands such as locating and replacing text, moving blocks of text, executing shell commands, and reading text from another file.

The relationship between command, edit, and extended command modes is depicted in Figure 3.3. Command mode is entered when **vi** is executed and when either of the other two modes is exited. Edit mode is entered from command mode when the user issues one of the edit commands, which append or insert new text and replace existing text. Edit mode is exited when the user presses `<ESC>`. Extended command mode is entered from command mode when the user types a colon (`:`), a slash (`/`), a question mark (`?`), or a double exclamation point (`!!`). Extended commands require more typing than the simple commands available in command mode. This mode is exited when the user presses `<CR>` and the command is carried out. The user exits from **vi** from command mode with or without saving the edit buffer.

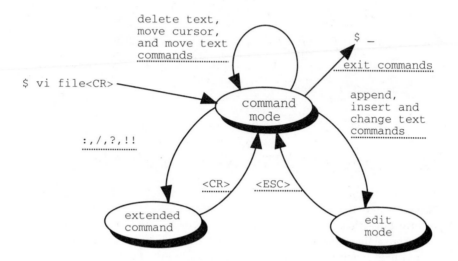

Figure 3.3: The relationship between **vi**'s command, edit, and extended
command modes

3.6   Moving the Cursor and Window

vi provides a variety of commands for positioning the cursor and moving
the edit window. These commands, effective only when **vi** is in command
mode, are summarized in Table 3.1 and described in the following sections.

3.6.1   Moving the Cursor

The four basic cursor-movement keys are h, j, k, and l. These keys move
the cursor one character to the left, down, up, and right, respectively, from
the current cursor position. Moving the cursor up or down positions it in the
same column on the preceding or subsequent line unless that column doesn't
exist, that is, unless that line is shorter than the current line. Moving
the cursor up from the top line or down from the bottom line of the edit
window moves the window up or down one line as well. Figure 3.4 depicts
the behavior of these commands. The cursor cannot be moved to the left
beyond the first character or to the right beyond the last character of the

Command	Effect
h	Move cursor left one character
l	Move cursor right one character
k	Move cursor up one line
j	Move cursor down one line
w	Move cursor to start of next word
b	Move cursor to first character of current or previous word
e	Move cursor to last character of current or next word
^	Move cursor to first non-whitespace character of current line
0	Move cursor to first character of current line including whitespace
$	Move cursor to last character of current line
-	Move cursor to first non-whitespace character of previous line
+	Move cursor to first non-whitespace character of next line
<CR>	Move cursor to first non-whitespace character of next line
H	Move cursor to first non-whitespace character of line at top of window
M	Move cursor to first non-whitespace character of line at center of window
L	Move cursor to first non-whitespace character of line at bottom of window
(	Move cursor to start of next sentence
)	Move cursor to end of current sentence
{	Move cursor to start of next paragraph
}	Move cursor to end of current paragraph
nG	Move cursor/window to line n of the file
G	Move cursor/window to the last line of the file
<CTRL-d>	Scroll window forward a half screen
<CTRL-u>	Scroll window backward a half screen
<CTRL-f>	Scroll window forward a full screen
<CTRL-b>	Scroll window backward a full screen

Table 3.1: Cursor-movement commands

current line and it cannot be moved up from the first line or down from the last line in the buffer.

Note 3.1 *On many terminals the arrow keys work as expected and may be used instead of the keys described here. However, some terminals and terminal emulators will not work as expected.*

The w key moves the cursor right to the first character of the next word. Typing a b moves the cursor left to the first character of the current or previous word, depending on the position of the cursor. If the cursor is positioned at the first character of the current word, b moves it to the first character of the previous word. Otherwise, the cursor is moved to the first

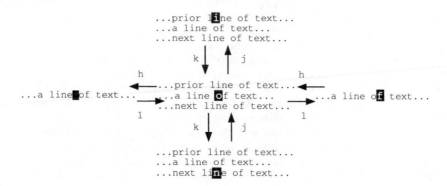

Figure 3.4: Left, down, up, and right cursor-movement keys

character of the current word. Figure 3.5 depicts the action of these two keys.

The **e** key is similar to **b** except that it moves the cursor right to the end of the current or next word. If the cursor is positioned at the last character of the current word, **e** moves it to the last character of the next word. Otherwise, the cursor is moved to the last character of the current word.

Unlike the left and right commands, these commands can move the cursor beyond the current line. The **w** and **e** keys advance the cursor from the last word of the current line to the appropriate position in the first word of the next line. The **b** key moves the cursor from the first word of the current line to the last word of the previous line. However, these commands cannot move the cursor beyond the first or last lines of the buffer.

The ^ key positions the cursor at the first non-whitespace character of the current line. Pressing a $ moves the cursor to the last character of the current line including whitespace. Figure 3.6 demonstrates the ^ and $ keys.

The 0 key complements the $ command. It moves the cursor to the first character of the current line including whitespace characters.

The − and + keys move the cursor up and down respectively. These commands differ from **k** and **j** in that instead of retaining the column position, the cursor moves to the first non-whitespace character of the appropriate

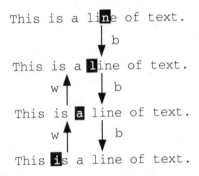

Figure 3.5: Word forward and backward cursor-movement keys

line. Figure 3.7 shows the behavior of these commands.

The <CR> key has the same effect as the + key.

The H, M, and L keys position the cursor relative to the edit window. The H key moves the cursor to the first line of the window—M and L position the cursor at the center and last lines of the window, respectively. In each case, the cursor is positioned at the first non-whitespace character. If the target line is empty or contains only whitespace, the cursor is positioned at the first whitespace character. Figure 3.8 demonstrates the action of H, M, and L.

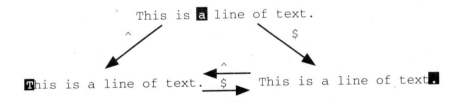

Figure 3.6: Beginning- and end-of-line cursor-movement keys

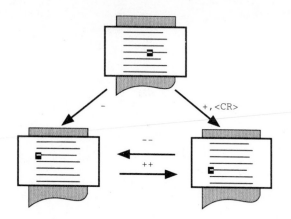

Figure 3.7: Additional up and down cursor-movement commands

The ⟨, ⟩, {, and } position the cursor with respect to *sentences* and *paragraphs*. A sentence is a sequence of words terminated with a period (.), an exclamation point (!), or a question mark (?). A paragraph is a sequence of sentences terminated by an empty line. The (and) keys move the cursor forward and backward through the buffer by sentences. A) positions the cursor at the first character of the next sentence, while (positions it at the first character of the previous sentence. These keys also treat the end of a paragraph as the end of a sentence. The { and } keys move the cursor forward and backward from paragraph to paragraph. A } key moves the cursor forward to the next paragraph and{ moves it backward. Like the other commands, these commands cannot move the cursor beyond the first or last lines of the buffer.

The G command positions the cursor by line number. Typing nG positions the cursor at the first non-whitespace character of line n. Typing G by itself places the cursor on the last line of the file. Figure 3.9 demonstrates the behavior of this command.

Note 3.2 *The effect of many of the cursor-movement commands is augmented by preceding them with a positive integer called a* multiplier. *In effect, the command is repeated* multiplier *times. For example,* 5j *moves the cursor down five lines,* 4w *advances the cursor by four words,* 3{ *moves the cursor backward by three paragraphs, and so forth.*

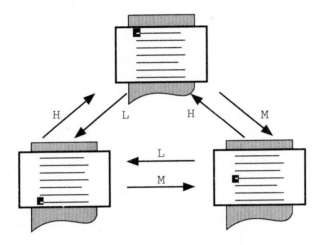

Figure 3.8: Top, center, and bottom-of-window cursor-movement keys

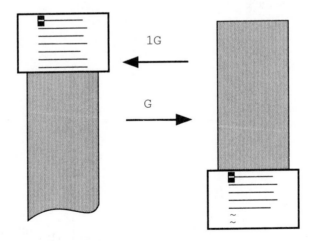

Figure 3.9: Go-to-line-number cursor-movement command

3.6.2 Moving the Window

This section describes commands that focus on positioning of the edit window. A side effect of these commands is that the cursor also moves when necessary, but their primary purpose is moving the window.

The <CTRL-d> and <CTRL-u> keys scroll the window forward and backward one half of the window's height, respectively. If the height of the window is 24 lines. <CTRL-d> scrolls the window forward 12 lines—<CTRL-u> scrolls the window backward 12 lines. These commands are depicted in Figure 3.10.

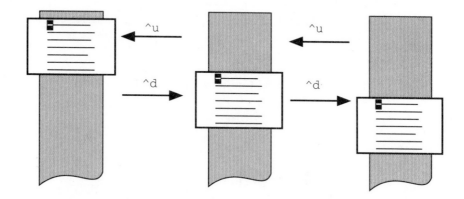

Figure 3.10: Scroll window forward and backward by half height

Similarly <CTRL-f> and <CTRL-b> scroll the screen forward and backward the full height of the window. The <CTRL-f> command positions the cursor in the upper left-hand corner of the window—<CTRL-b> places the cursor in the lower left-hand corner. Figure 3.11 indicates the behavior of these keys.

3.7 Appending and Inserting Text

This section describes the *append*, *insert*, and *open* commands used to add new text to the edit buffer. Table 3.2 summarizes these commands.

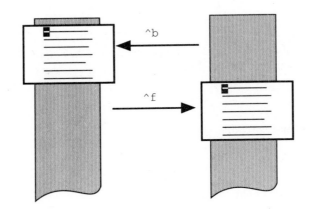

Figure 3.11: Scroll window forward and backward by full height

Command	Effect
a*text*<ESC>	Append *text* after cursor
A*text*<ESC>	Append *text* at end of line
i*text*<ESC>	Insert *text* before cursor
I*text*<ESC>	Insert *text* before first non-whitespace character
o*text*<ESC>	Open new line after current line and insert *text*
O*text*<ESC>	Open new line before current line and insert *text*

Table 3.2: Append and insert commands

3.7.1 Append Text

The append text command, invoked by typing a, adds text to the buffer immediately after the current position of the cursor. To illustrate:

```
A_stone gathers ...
+
arolling <ESC>
↓
A rolling_stone gathers ...
```

Another form of append, initiated by pressing the A key, appends text after the end of the current line as follows:

```
A rolling stone gathers
+
A no moss<ESC>
↓
A rolling stone gathers no moss
```

3.7.2   Insert Text

The insert command adds text before the cursor's current position. This command is invoked by typing i followed by the text to be inserted. For example:

```
Peter Piper a peck
+
ipicked <ESC>
↓
Peter Piper picked_a peck
```

A variation of the insert command inserts text before the first non-whitespace character of the current line. This command is invoked with the I key as follows:

```
Piper picked ...
+
IPeter <ESC>
↓
Peter_Piper picked ...
```

Note 3.3 *When appending or inserting several lines of text, remember that visual wraparound occurs if the current line exceeds the width of the screen. However,* **vi** *does not insert carriage returns—you must explicitly insert these with the* <CR> *key.*

3.7.3 Open New Line

The open commands insert text by opening a new line directly above or below the current line. The o command inserts text into a new line directly below the current line. For example:

```
Peter Piper picked a peck
+
oof pickled peppers<ESC>
↓
Peter Piper picked a peck
of pickled peppers
```

The second command, O, inserts the text into a new line before the current line. For instance:

```
Peter Piper picked a peck
+
Oof pickled peppers<ESC>
↓
of pickled peppers
Peter Piper picked a peck
```

Note 3.4 *Multipliers do not work with append, insert, and open commands.*

3.8   Changing, Replacing and Substituting Text

The *change*, *replace*, and *substitute* commands, summarized in Table 3.3, provide a means of modifying and replacing existing text. In general, these commands allow the user to change or replace a specified scope of text— characters, words, lines, and so forth. If the text typed by the user exceeds the specified scope, **vi** adds the text in a fashion similar to the append and insert commands. For example, a single word may be replaced by several new lines of text. However, some of the replace commands, notably replace character, limit modifications to the specified scope.

Command	Effect
c*nwtext*<ESC>	Change *n* words to *text*
C*text*<ESC>	Change through the end of line to *text*
*n*cc*text*<ESC>	Change *n* lines to *text*
rα	Replace current character with α
R*text*<ESC>	Replace typed over characters with *text*
s*text*	Substitute *text* for character at cursor position
S*text*	Substitute *text* for current line

Table 3.3: Change, replace, and substitute commands

3.8.1 Change Word

The change word command, `cw`, changes the current word or portion of a word to user-supplied text. The text from the cursor's position up to the end of the current word is replaced with new text typed by the user. For example:

```
incredulous edibles ...
+
cwible<ESC>
↓
incredible edibles ...
```

Unlike append, insert, and open commands, multipliers can be used with this command. The syntax is:

```
cnwtext<ESC>
```

vi changes n words, starting from the cursor's position, to *text*. Thus c2wdee dee changes the next two words to dee dee:

```
Hi diddle da da
+
c2wdee dee<ESC>
↓
Hi diddle dee dee
```

3.8.2 Change Line

Two commands change a partial line or series of lines. The change to end of line command, `C`, changes the current line from the cursor's position to the end of the line. For example:

```
How much leather can a leather chuck chuck
+
Cwood can a wood chuck chuck <ESC>
↓
How much wood can a wood chuck chuck_
```

The change line change command, cc, changes the current line. Regardless of the cursor position, this command replaces the entire current line with text typed by the user.

```
A funny thing happened
+
ccon the way to the forum<ESC>
↓
on the way to the forum
```

Multipliers also apply to the cc command. The command:

ncc text<ESC>

replaces *n* lines, starting at the current line, with *text*.

3.8.3 Replace Character

Replace character, r, replaces the character at the cursor position with one typed by the user. The effect is multiplied by typing an integer before the r. For example:

```
A wird in hand
+
rb
↓
A bird in hand
```

replaces **w** with **b** while typing **5rb** has the following effect:

```
A wird in hand
+
5rb
↓
A bbbbbin hand
```

3.8.4 Replace Characters

Replace characters, **R**, is a variation of the **r** command. With this command, all characters typed over by the user are replaced until <ESC> is pressed or the end of the line is reached. If the end of line is reached, additional text is added similar to an append command. For example:

```
If at first you don't succeed
+
Rlast you finally <ESC>
↓
If at last you finally_succeed
```

A multiplier cannot be applied to the **R** command.

3.8.5   Substitute Commands

The substitute commands replace existing characters and append new text.
The s command substitutes text typed by the user for the character at the
cursor position. This is similar to the r command except the user is not
limited to replacing a single character. A single character can be replaced
with words, lines, or even paragraphs. For example:

```
The early bird is the worm ...
                  ‾‾
+
sget<ESC>
↓
The early bird gets the worm
                  ‾‾
```

A multiplier works with the s command so that:

```
ns text<ESC>
```

replaces *n* characters, starting with the one marked by the cursor, with the
supplied *text*. Thus:

```
The early bird snags the worm
               ‾
+
4sget<ESC>
↓
The early bird gets the worm
                  ‾‾
```

The S command is a variation of the s command. This command substitutes text typed by the user for the current line, that is, it has the same
effect as the cc command.

3.9 Deleting Text

vi provides several commands that delete characters, words, lines, sentences, and paragraphs of text. Table 3.4 summarizes these commands, which are described in the following sections. Each of these commands, except D, operates with a multiplier. If the multiplier is omitted, it assumes a default value of 1. Furthermore, the deleted text is placed in an anonymous buffer that can be referenced by the commands described in Section 3.10.

Command	Effect
*n*x	Delete *n* characters
*n*d<SPACE>	Delete *n* characters
*n*dw	Delete *n* words
*n*dd	Delete *n* lines
D	Delete to end of line
*n*d)	Delete *n* sentences
*n*d}	Delete *n* paragraphs

Table 3.4: Text deletion commands

Note 3.5 *The descriptions in this section refer to the syntax presented in Table 3.4. However, in several cases the syntax* dnα *is synonymous with* ndα.

3.9.1 Delete Character

The delete character command, x, deletes the character at the cursor's position. For example:

```
dofgs
+
x
↓
dogs
```

Several consecutive characters, up to the end of the current line, are deleted by preceding x with a multiplier. For example, 5x deletes five consecutive characters starting at the cursor's position. The command 55x deletes 55 characters or until the end of the line is reached—x cannot delete more characters than appear on the current line. Finally note that d followed by a space, that is, "d ", acts like an x command.

3.9.2   Delete Word

Delete word, dw, deletes characters from the cursor's position up to the start of the next word. For example:

```
Now is the time for all men ...
+
dw
↓
Now is the time all men ...
```

If the cursor is positioned in the middle of a word, the remainder of the word and all whitespace up until the start of the next word is deleted. For example:

```
Whenever I feel like exercising, I lie down until the feeling passes
+
dw
↓
WhenI feel like exercising, I lie down until the feeling passes
```

Like all other delete commands, delete word can be preceded by a multiplier. For example 10dw deletes 10 words starting with the one pointed to by the cursor.

3.9.3   Delete Line

The delete line command, dd, deletes the current line. For example:

```
Now is the time for all men to
come to the aid of their party.
+
dd
↓
Now is the time for all men to

_
```

Multiple lines are deleted by preceding this command with a multiplier. Thus 100dd deletes 100 lines starting with the current line.

3.9.4 Delete to End of Line

The delete to end of line command, D, deletes text from the cursor's position up to the end of the line. For example:

```
Now is the time for all men to
+
D
↓
Now is the time_
```

3.9.5 Delete Sentence and Paragraph

The delete sentence and paragraph commands delete text from the cursor's position up to the end of the current sentence or paragraph. Delete sentence, d), behaves as follows:

```
Now is the time for all
men to come to the aid of their party.
+
d)
↓
Now is the time_
```

Similarly, the current paragraph is deleted from the point of the cursor by typing d}. Both of these commands span multiple lines as needed.

Note 3.6 **vi** *remembers the latest append, insert, change, replace, substitute, or delete command and the modifications it caused to the edit buffer. This information is used by the* undo *and* repeat *commands. The undo command allows the user to reverse the most recent change to the buffer— new text is removed from and deleted text returned to the buffer. The repeat command allows the user to repeat the latest modification.*

3.10   Moving and Copying Text

Moving and copying text involves the delete commands, summarized in Table 3.4, as well as the *yank* and *put* commands. The yank and put commands, summarized in Table 3.5, are described in the following sections.

3.10.1   Moving Text with Delete and Put Commands

The delete commands place the removed text into a temporary memory buffer called a *register*. The put command, p, inserts the content of this register into the edit buffer, that is, into the file, after the current line or the cursor's position. If the register contains a line or series of lines, perhaps deleted with the dd command, the text is inserted after the current line. Otherwise, the text is inserted into the current line immediately after the cursor. For example, the dd command immediately followed by the p command exchanges two lines. The dd command deletes a line, places it into the temporary register, and positions the cursor on the subsequent line. The p command inserts the line from the register after the current line. Consider the following example:

Command	Effect
p	Put text from the temporary register after the cursor
np	Put n copies of the temporary register after the cursor
P	Put text from the temporary register before the cursor
yw	Yank current word into the temporary register
yy	Yank current line into the temporary register
Y	Same as yy
y$	Yank from cursor to end of line into the temporary register
y)	Yank sentence into the temporary register
y}	Yank paragraph into the temporary register
nyα	Yank n copies of α into the temporary register

Table 3.5: Move and copy commands

```
Better, let sleeping dogs lie.
Let lying dogs sleep.
+
ddp
↓
Let lying dogs sleep.
Better, let sleeping dogs lie.
```

As another example, the two-character command combination xp exchanges two characters. The x command deletes the character at the cursor and places it in the temporary register, moving the cursor to the next character. p inserts the first back into into the line after the cursor as follows:

```
recieve
+
xp
↓
```

```
rece_ive
```

Text can be moved or copied with just the delete and put commands. To move text, position the cursor at the source text, delete it, move the cursor to the destination position, and put it into the file. Copying text is essentially the same—move the cursor to the source text, delete it, restore it by putting it back into its original position, and copy it to the appropriate positions in the file. This is a simple, brute-force, commonly used way to move and copy text.

3.10.2   Copying Text with Yank and Put Commands

Yank commands copy text objects into the temporary register without deleting them. These commands, used in combination with put commands, allow the user to copy text a bit more gracefully than with delete commands. Each yank command starts with the letter y and ends with an object specifier. The yank word command, yw, copies text from the cursor's position up to the end of the current word into the temporary register. The commands y\$, y), and y} copy text from the cursor up to the end of the line, the end of the sentence, and the end of the paragraph, respectively. The yy command copies the entire current line into the register regardless of the cursor position. Since these commands do not delete their respective text objects, yank commands cannot be used to move text.

Multiple objects are copied by preceding the yank command with a multiplier. For instance, 5yy yanks the current line and four subsequent lines into the temporary register. All five lines are output by subsequent put commands.

3.10.3   Using Named Registers

vi provides named registers that work with delete, yank, and put commands to move and copy text in much the same way as the temporary register. However, unlike the temporary register, the content of a named register is not automatically altered by delete and yank commands. The temporary register's content is replaced with each delete or yank command. A named register's content is altered only when the user references it—once a named register is loaded with some text, its content remains intact until the user references it again. This feature allows temporary storage of multiple text objects and makes copying text much more convenient.

There is a named register corresponding to each of the lowercase letters, that is, there are 26 named registers—a through z. A named register is referred to by preceding the register's name with a double quote mark ("). Therefore, "a refers to register a, "b refers to register b, and so forth.

A named register is used in conjunction with a delete, yank, or put command by preceding the command with a reference to the desired register. For example, "ayy yanks the current line into register a, "byw places a copy of the current word into register b, and "cdd deletes the current line placing it into both register c and the temporary register. The command "ap inserts the content of register a into the file immediately following the cursor. Table 3.6 summarizes the use of named registers.

Command	Effect
"αp	Put from named buffer α
"αdβ	Delete object β and place in named buffer α
"αyβ	Yank object β and place in named buffer α

Table 3.6: Using named registers

3.11 Exiting vi – Write and Quit

The *write* command writes the edit buffer to files, and the *quit* command exits **vi**. These commands are summarized in Table 3.7.

Command	Effect
w<CR>	Write buffer to file
w *newfile*<CR>	Write buffer to *newfile*
wq<CR>	Write buffer to file and exit
ZZ	Same as :wq
x,yw *file*	Write lines n through y to *file*
q<CR>	Quit — exit if no changes made
q!<CR>	Quit — exit and abandon any changes made

Table 3.7: Write and quit commands

3.11.1   Saving Changes

The write command, **w**, writes the edit buffer to a file. By default, it writes
the buffer to the file that was used to load the edit buffer. This command
is issued from extended command mode so it must be preceded by a colon
(:) (remember that from command mode **w** is the word forward command).
Therefore, changes are saved to the file as follows:

`:w<CR>`

After the file is saved, **vi** returns to command mode.

   To save changes and exit, issue a write command followed by a quit
command as follows:

`:wq<CR>`

A short cut for this command, from command mode, is **ZZ**.

Note 3.7 *It is a good idea during a long editing session to save changes
periodically (say every five minutes). The write command can be issued at
any time and it doesn't take very long. This practice can protect you from
losing hours of work when the power fails or some other catastrophe befalls
the system!*

3.11.2   Writing the Buffer to a New File

The write command creates new files as follows:

`:w` *newfile*

where *newfile* is the name or pathname of the file to be created with the
content of the edit buffer.

   Occasionally the user wants to write out sections of the edit buffer for
debugging purposes or to include them as an insert to another file. This is
accomplished by specifying a range of line numbers to the write command:

`:`x, y `w` *newfile*`<CR>`

vi writes the buffer lines x through y to the file specified by *newfile*. For example, suppose the user wants to write out line 10 to line 30 to a file called `temp`. This is done as follows:

`:10,30w temp<CR>`

3.11.3 Exiting vi

The quit command, `q`, exits **vi**. This command is also issued from extended command mode so it must be preceded by a colon. To exit when there are no unsaved changes to the edit buffer, issue the quit command as follows:

`:q<CR>`

If changes to the buffer have been made and not saved, **vi** prevents the user from exiting until the changes are saved or the user insists on abandoning them. Changes to the edit buffer are abandoned as follows:

`:q!<CR>`

3.12 Searching for Text

vi provides several commands that position the cursor by searching through the buffer for specified text or text patterns. These commands can search for a single character, a string of characters, or a pattern that matches any of a number of strings. The cursor can be placed to the left or the right of the target string. In addition, searches may be conducted forward or backward and reversed if needed. The search commands are summarized in Table 3.8.

3.12.1 Search for Character

The `f`, `F`, `t`, and `T` commands search for single characters within the current line using different strategies. The `f` command searches for the specified character from the cursor's position to the right up to the end of the current line. For example, `fx` moves the cursor to the right until it encounters the first `x`. The `F` command is similar except it searches to the left of the cursor's position. Therefore, `Fx` searches to the left for the first `x`. Both of these commands position the cursor at the target character.

The `t` and `T` commands work exactly like their counterparts `f` and `F` except that the cursor is positioned either immediately prior to or after the target character—`t` positions the cursor prior to the target, `T` positions the cursor after the target. The `;` command repeats the previous `f` or `F` command within the same line.

Command	Effect
fα	Move cursor right to character α
Fα	Move cursor left to character α
tα	Move cursor right and position it prior to character α
Tα	Move cursor left and position it after to character α
;	Repeat previous f or F command
/*text*/	Search forward for the first occurrence of *text*
?*text*?	Search backward for the first occurrence of *text*
n	Repeat previous / or ? command
N	Repeat previous / or ? command in reverse direction
//	Repeat previous / or ? command
??	Repeat previous / or ? command in reverse direction

Table 3.8: Search commands

3.12.2   Word Searching

The / and ? search throughout the buffer for strings containing one or more characters. The / command searches forward through the buffer and ? searches backward. Note that these commands are not limited to the current line or constrained by the top or bottom of the file. For example, searching forward includes wrapping around from the last character of the current line to the first column of the next line and continuing the search. If the end of the file is encountered, the search continues with the first character of the first line. Searching backward behaves similarly. If the start of line is encountered and the target character or string is not found, the search continues with the last character of the previous line. If the start of file is encountered without finding the character, the search continues with the last character in the file.

For example, the command /egg searches forward through the file for the first occurrence of the string egg. Similarly, ?egg searches backwards through the file for the same string.

Either command can be repeated with the n or N command. Typing n repeats the previous search, whether forward or backward, in the same direction. Typing /egg followed by n searches forward from the cursor's position and locates the first and second occurrences of the string egg. Typing /egg followed by N initially searches forward for egg and then reverses direction to search backward through the file. A ? command followed by N initially searches backward and then reverses to search forward. Note that the // and ?? commands are analogous to n and N respectively.

3.12.3   Find and Substitute

vi allows the user to find and replace strings very easily. Find and substitution is performed by; entering extended command mode, supplying a range of lines within which to conduct the search, specifying the text to be replaced, and finally, supplying the replacement text. Generically the command looks like:

`:` *start, end***s/** *text***/** *new text*`[/[g]]<CR>`

vi searches the buffer from line *start* through line *end* for the string *text*. If found, *text* is replaced with *new text*. Otherwise, **vi** indicates that the pattern was not matched, that is, it could not find *text*.

The *start* and *end* range specifiers may refer to explicit lines, the current line, the last line, or to a line relative to the current line. Lines are referred to explicitly by line number, that is, by an integer from 1 to n where n is the number of lines in the file. The current line is referred to by a period (.). The last line is denoted by a dollar sign ($). Lines relative to the current line are referred to as follows:

`:-m,+n`

where `-m` refers to the mth line prior to the current line and `+n` refers to the nth line subsequent to the current line. If *start* or *end* are omitted, they default to the current line and when present, the line referred to by *start* must precede the line referred to by *end*. Table 3.9 summarizes the range specifications for the find and substitute command.

Find and substitute commands replace the first occurrence of the target string *text* with *new text* in each line that is both within the range and in which the target string appears. For example, the following command searches from the current line through the end of the file, replacing the first occurrence of the number 6 with the word **six** in each line in which it appears:

`:.,$s/ 6 / six /<CR>`

Command	Effect
m,n	Search lines m through n.
$m,+n$	Search lines m through current line $+n$.
$-m,$	Search current line $-m$ through current line.
.,$+m$	Search current line to current line $+m$.
.,\$	Search current line to end of file.
1,\$	Search first line of file to end of file.
%	Search entire file.

Table 3.9: Range specifications for the find and substitute command

Note that the digit **6** is surrounded by blanks to prevent it from being replaced in the middle of a number like **263**. Regardless of the number of occurrences of a **6** within a line, only the first occurrence in each line is replaced. Furthermore, if there are no occurrences between the current line and end of file, then no substitutions are made.

As a second example, suppose the string **good** is to be replaced with **great** the first time it appears in each of the lines between **10** and **50**. This is accomplished as follows:

```
:10,50s/good/great/<CR>
```

To replace every occurrence of the target string within the range, a **/g** is appended to the command. This argument instructs **vi** to make the substitution globally within each line, that is, perform substitution for all occurrences in a line. For example:

```
:1,$s/analyse/analyze/g<CR>
```

substitutes **analyze** for **analyse** everywhere in the file. In contrast:

```
:1,$s/analyse/analyze/<CR>
```

performs the substitution only for the first occurrence of `analyse` in each line of the file. Finally, to replace the word `cat` with the word `dog` for every occurrence within 50 lines of the current line, type

```
:-50,+50s/cat/dog/g<CR>
```

3.12.4 Regular Expressions

Regular expressions, constructed from special characters called *meta-characters*, expand the ordinary search and/or substitution strategies previously discussed to allow for more complex searches. Meta-characters, summarized in Table 3.10, and their use in regular expressions are illustrated by several search examples in this section. Their use in find and substitute commands is similar.

Command	Effect
\>	End of word indicator
\<	Start of word indicator
[ ]	Character class definition
ˆ	Match beginning of line
$	Match end of line
.	Match any single character
*	Match 0 or more occurrences of preceding character
[ˆ]	Match any character except those listed
l–u	Lexical range *l* to *u* within character class

Table 3.10: Meta-characters used in regular expressions

The following expression locates the first occurence of a word ending in `ing`:

```
/ing\><CR>
```

To locate the next occurance of a word starting with `The` or `Thy`, the following expression is used:

```
/\<Th[ey]
```

To find the next occurance of a line ending with **again**:

```
/again$
```

To find the next occurrence of a line starting with **Once**, use:

```
/^Once<CR>
```

Character classes allow moderately sophisticated searches. For example, the locate the next occurrence of a word starting with a vowel:

```
/\<[aeiouAEIOU]<CR>
```

In contrast, to locate the next occurrence of any word starting with a consonant:

```
/\<[^aeiouAEIOU]
```

The period (.) and asterisk (*) provide a great deal of flexibility. The period matches any single character. The asterisk matches 0 or more occurrences of the character preceding it. Therefore, the expression:

```
/\<ha.<CR>
```

matches any three-letter word starting with **ha**. The pattern:

```
/\<ha*<CR>
```

matches any word starting with the letter **h** followed by 0 or more of the character **a**. To match any word starting with **ha**, the following pattern is used:

```
/\<ha.*<CR>
```

and to match any word consisting of **h** followed by 1 or more of the character **a**:

```
/\<haa*
```

Finally, to find any word starting with **h** followed by 1 or more **a**s:

```
/\<haa*.*<CR>
```

As suggested, regular expressions can also be used with string search and replacement. For example, to locate all occurrences of words ending with **ts** and replace the ending with **ing**:

```
:%s/ts\>/ing/g
```

To locate all lines beginning with an **a** and replace the first letter with **A**:

```
:%s/^a/A/
```

Regular expressions are commonly used and best learned by practice. They undoubtedly will become part of your tool-set as you become more experienced.

3.13   Reversing Mistakes

The **vi** editor provides protection against an erroneous or unwanted change through the use of two undo commands. These commands permit you to reverse the last command that actually changed the contents of the edit buffer. These commands are summarized in Table 3.11.

Command	Effect
u	Undo the last command
U	Return current line to its initial state

Table 3.11: Undo commands

The first of these, the undo command, is invoked simply by pressing the u key. The effect of this command is that the previous command that changed the edit buffer will be undone. If the undo is pressed twice, then the undo is undone. Thus the edit buffer will be the same as it was before

the first undone was executed. Please note that **vi** does not keep a history
of all changes made—it only saves the changes to the current line and a
history of deleted lines. These are the only changes that can be undone.

The second undo key, U, will return a line to its unmolested state after
making a series of changes if the cursor is not moved from that line. This
is particularly useful if after a series of changes to a line of text with which
you are not happy, you wish to return it to its original form. For example,
suppose a line of text in your file is the following:

```
now is the time for all men to come to the aid of their country
```

and suppose after making several changes to the line it appears as:

```
now is not the time for all young men to come to the aid of there country
```

executing the U command will return the line to its original form. Unlike
the **u** command, the U command cannot undo itself.

3.14   Programmer Aids

Because **vi** was written for the Unix operating system, and is closely associated with C, it has several features that are designed to make life easier
for C programmers.

3.14.1   Autoindent Mode

A well-written C program is properly indented according to the rules given
to you by your text or instructor. While the C-beautifier program (**cb**
discussed in chapter 4) can automatically indent a program after it has been
written, it is nice to indent the program as it is being created. **vi** provides
a special autoindent mode to facilitate this. To put **vi** in autoindent mode,
type the command

```
:set autoindent
```

Once invoked, autoindent automatically provides enough white space while
in insert mode to align a new line with the previous line. You can tab to
the next indentation position by typing <CTRL-t>. To cancel the automatic

indentation for one level, that is to tab back, type `<CTRL-d>`. You can use `<CTRL-d>` to cancel as many levels as needed to align the closing } with the opening {.

Autoindent can be canceled at any time by typing the command

```
:set noautoindent
```

3.14.2   Showmatch Mode

Another **vi** feature that helps in the preparation of programs allows the user to set a parameter that tells **vi** to show the opening {, (, or [, when the corresponding closing bracket is typed. In this mode, **vi** moves the cursor from the closing character to its mate and back again. The feature is activated by typing the command

```
:set showmatch
```

The command is invoked simply by typing the closing bracket corresponding to the opening bracket of the one you want to find.

This feature is useful for searching for mismatched parentheses and braces or for checking a deeply nested set of loops or branch statements.

The feature can be disabled by typing the command

```
:set noshowmatch
```

If you wish to include both autoindentation and showmatch mode in every **vi** session, you can set the appropriate parameters in your `.profile` file. To do so, add the commands

```
EXINIT='set ai sm'
export EXINIT
```

to `.profile`. To enable only one feature, include the appropriate string **ai** or **sm** only in `.profile` for autoindent and showmatch respectively.

3.15   Miscellaneous Editing Features

We close this chapter with a discussion of other editing features that you
might find useful.

3.15.1   Editing Multiple Files

Suppose you have begun a **vi** edit session on file `apple.c` and after making
changes (and saving them with the `w` command) you wish to edit another
file, say `pear.c`. From the command line, invoked by typing : you can type
`e pear.c` to replace the edit buffer with `pear.c`! Is `apple.c` out of the edit
buffer? No it is still "in reserve," sort of in the way depicted in Figure 3.12.
You can thus switch between `apple.c` and `pear.c` by typing `:e#`, so long
as you save any changes in between.

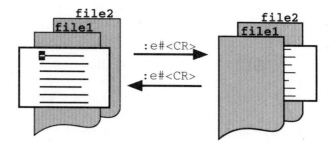

Figure 3.12: Editing two files

More than two files can be edited in **vi**. To facilitate this, **vi** allows the
user to place several edit files in a list so that they can be edited sequentially.
For example,

```
$ vi *.c
```

will cause all the files in the current directory that end in a `.c` extension
to be made available to the editor, although only the lexicographically first
file will be loaded into the edit buffer. The remaining files queue for editing
as in Figure 3.13.

The files can only be edited one at a time and must be saved before the next file can be edited. You can edit the next file in the lexicographic list by typing the :n command.

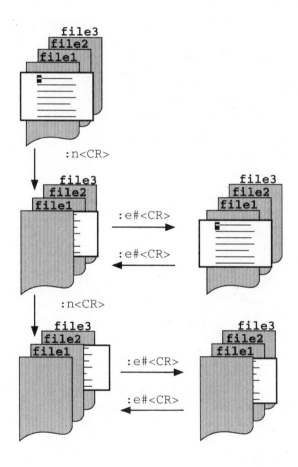

Figure 3.13: Editing multiple files

Another way to edit multiple files is to type:

```
$ vi file1 file2 ... filen
```

In this case the files line up for editing as in Figure 3.13, and the :n command works to sequence through these files as before.

Note 3.8 *If you wish to end an editing session in which you specified several files but didn't edit all of them, you must use a* wq! *to save the current file and leave or* q! *to leave, even if you made no changes—try it.*

3.15.2   Escape to Shell

A nice feature of the **vi** editor is the ability to escape to the shell, that is, temporarily leave the editor and perform some command, then return to the edit session as if you never left. Escaping to the shell is accomplished by typing

```
:!sh<CR>
```

or

```
:shell<CR>
```

or

```
:sh<CR>
```

where you will receive the familiar Unix prompt. To return to the edit session you must exit the shell as if you are logging off (type <CTRL-d> or **exit**). (You can exit to the shell for a single command by typing :!command).

3.15.3   Reading In Files

During the edit process, you may wish to insert the contents of other files into the current edit buffer. When writing C programs, for example, you may wish to begin your program by inserting a boiler-plate template at the beginning of the program. **vi** allows you to do this with the r or read file command.

Suppose you wish to include file `template.c` in your program file. Simply place the cursor at the line above the point of insertion and type `:r template.c`. The file will then be inserted immediately after the cursor. If you know the specific line number where you wish to insert the file, you can specify that too. For example, if file `junk` is to be inserted at line 43, you can type `:42r junk`. Note that the line specified is the one before the point of insertion because **vi** will insert the file after the specified line number.

3.15.4 Recovering Edits Lost at Hangup

Occasionally during the course of an editing session, a catastrophe will strike, such as a power failure, or a system crash. If you were unable to save your editing session before this event, then all of your changes are lost. Right? Maybe not. **vi** provides a recovery parameter at the command prompt that may allow an edit session to be recovered.

Suppose you were editing file `foobar.c` when your friend tripped over your terminal and pulled out the plug. The operating system may, after a period of time, determine the terminal is abandoned and log you off the system. Fortunately, however, it may save your editing session before this. To see if this was done, log back on and type:

```
$ vi -r
```

The `-r` option to the **vi** command will list all (if any) of the recovery files available in your directory. These should have a name similar to the file that you were editing but with a `.r` appended. Once the existence of such a file has been established, the edit session can be recovered by typing:

```
$ vi -r file
```

where *file* is the name of the file that was being edited during the interruption.

3.15.5 Other Miscellaneous Features

There are other commands which the casual **vi** user may also find useful. These are neatly summarized in Table 3.12

Command	Effect
.	Repeat last command
J	Join the current and next line together
\<CTRL-v\>	Print out non-printing character
\<CTRL-l\>	Clear and redraw screen
~	Change upper case to lower case and *vice versa*
:	Enter command line mode

Table 3.12: Miscellaneous commands

3.16   Exercises

1. Define the following terms:

    (a) edit buffer

    (b) edit window

    (c) cursor

    (d) command mode

    (e) edit mode

    (f) command line

    (g) register

2. For what commands discussed in this chapter do multipliers work? For which do they not?

3. Describe the effects of the following commands:

    (a) 5dd

    (b) ra

    (c) xp

    (d) cwcart

4. Name two **vi** commands to save and exit.

5. Find out if the `cc` or `C` commands can be preceded by a multiplier.

6. Using **vi**, create a file with the following text:

```
How much wood could a woodchuck chuck if a woodchuck could chuck wood
The big black bug bled black bug
Peter Piper picked a peck of pickled peppers
Unique New York
```

   (a) Exchange lines **1** and **4** of the file.

   (b) Change the word **chuck** to the **chew** using a single command.

   (c) Change **black bug** to **bug black** throughout.

   (d) Exit to the shell using `:!` and execute a simple **ls** command.

   (e) Write out only lines **3** and **4** of the file.

7. Edit your `.profile` file and use the shell command to escape to the shell. From the shell try a few commands, then return to the edit session.

8. Discuss two methods for editing multiple files.

9. Experiment with the **t**, **T**, and **;** commands.

10. Give a regular expression that can be used to find the next string in a file that begins with a single consonant and is followed by the string **ed**.

11. Give a regular expression that can be used to find the next line in a file that begins with the word **The**.

12. Give a **vi** command to search and replace the every occurrence of a word ending in **ing** and replace it with the ending **ed**.

Chapter 4

Compiling, Testing, and Debugging

In this chapter we discuss the basic C language compile command and the various ways to compile source files into executable programs. At the conclusion of this chapter you should be able to compile and run C language programs.

4.1   The Compiler

In general, a *compiler* translates a program from high-level source code language into relocatable machine instructions. Usually this process is broken into a series of phases.

First, the high-level language program is translated into a symbolic machine code form called *assembly language*. Next, a separate program called an *assembler* is used to translate the symbolic assembly language into relocatable *machine code* or *object code*. At some stage in the compilation process, *optimization* of the code may take place. Finally, the relocatable code output from the compiler is made absolute, and all external references are resolved, by a program called a *linker*, or *linking loader*. The overall process is illustrated in Figure 4.1. Once the program has been processed by the linker, it is ready for execution.

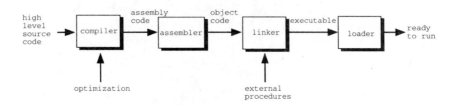

Figure 4.1: The compilation and linking processes

4.1.1   The Unix C Compiler

The Unix C compiler, **cc**, provides a utility that controls the compilation and linking processes. In subsequent sections of this chapter, we describe the use of **cc** to prepare source programs for execution.

In particular, in Unix System V version 3 (SVR3), the **cc** program provides for the following phases of compilation:

1. Preprocessing

2. Compilation

3. Optimization

4. Assembly

5. Linking and loading

These phases are illustrated in Figure 4.2 and summarized in Table 4.1.

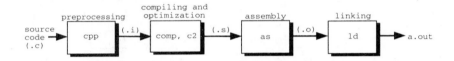

Figure 4.2: Phases of compilation provided by the **cc** compiler

Phase	Program
Preprocessing	**cpp**
Compilation	**ccom**
Optimization	**c2**
Assembly	**as**
Linking and loading	**ld**

Table 4.1: Phases of compilation and their associated program

These programs may have other names or be unavailable on systems, except for **cc** and **cpp**, that are found on all Unix implementations.

The preprocessing phase of the compiler, performed by the program **cpp**, takes care of such things as converting symbolic values into actual values and evaluating and expanding code macros.

The compilation of the program, that is, the translation of the program from C language to assembly language, is performed by the program **ccom**.

Optimization of the code is performed by the program **c2**, and assembly or translation of the assembly language code into machine codes is taken care of by **as**.

Finally, the object modules are linked together, all external references (for example library routines) are resolved, and the program (or an image of it) is loaded into memory by the program **ld**. The executable program is now ready to run!

The fact that many of these phases can be bypassed or run alone is an important feature that will help in program debugging and optimization.

4.1.2   Naming Conventions

Unix in general and C programmers in particular use certain conventions when naming C source code files and their various relations. Table 4.2 summarizes some of these conventions. Your text on the C language should

Extension	Meaning
.a	Archive library
.i	Source code with macros expanded
.c	C source file
.s	Assembly language code file
.o	Object code file
none	Executable file

Table 4.2: C program extension conventions and their meaning

describe these for you, but we will review them here. While many of these conventions can be superseded, it is strongly advised that this not be done.

C source code programs are always assumed to end in a .c extension. For example, `test.c`, `sort.c`, `game.c`, and so on. are all valid C source code file names. Include files are always given a .h extension. The output of the preprocessor, **cpp**, has a .i extension, the output of the compiler or optimizer has a .s extension, and the output of the assembler, **as**, has a .o extension. If not explicitly requested, many of these files are created and deleted invisibly to the user.

Finally, the output of the linker, **ld**, is the executable program file. The convention for executables is to have no extension, but by default **ld** produces an executable file called `a.out`. We will show you how to change the output so that it conforms to convention shortly.

Example 4.1 *You are preparing a C source program that performs a bubble* *sort. You might name this file* `bsort.c`. *Depending on the compiler options you choose, the following files would be associated with this program:*

- `bsort.i` – *the program with expanded macros*

- `bsort.s` – *the assembly language equivalent*

- `bsort.o` – *the object code*

- `bsort` – *the executable code*

We will describe how to create these associated files in the following sections.

4.2   The cc Command

The basic command syntax for invoking the C compiler and linking and loading your program is:

```
$ cc [options] filename(s)
```

The options, described in the next subsection, can come after the filenames if desired. The filename or names, can be either `.c`, `.s`, or `.o` files, which are C source code files, assembly language or object files respectively. If the file is a C source code file, then it is translated and linked with the other files. If the file is an `.s` file, it is assembled and linked. If the file is a `.o` file, it is just linked.

cc tells you the name of the filename it is processing (and some compilers tell you which procedures within the file it is processing as well). It also outputs warnings and errors. Finally, the **cc** program outputs file `a.out`. `a.out` is the executable file corresponding to the input files given. To execute this program, type:

```
$ a.out
```

To illustrate the method, suppose you wished to compile the complete source file `sort.c`, which contained a main program, and all procedures it referenced were either defined within or referenced through `#include` files. Then to compile simply type:

```
$ cc sort.c
```

You might see:

```
sort.c:
```

(and hopefully no errors or warnings). In addition, an executable file called `a.out` was created, that can be run in the manner previously discussed.

4.2.1   Options

The C compiler program, **cc**, has various options which allow you to bypass or suppress certain phases of the compilation process or allow you to specify certain output files. The option switches that we are about to discuss are succinctly described in Table 4.3.

Option	Effect
-P	Run preprocessor only. .i files are produced.
-c	Suppress the loading phase, **ld**. .o files are produced. Does not create executable file.
-o *name*	Executable file is named *name* instead of a.out.
-S	Produce assembly language code.
-O	Invoke the optimizer, **c2**.
-g	Produce symbol table needed by the debugger.
-I *pathname*	Specify pathnames for include files.
-l *pathname*	Specify libraries (and path) to be included during the link phase. This option must appear last.

Table 4.3: C compiler options and their meaning

The first option, -P, executes the preprocessor only. This has the effect of expanding all macros: that is, it converts all #defines to their numeric or C code equivalent and pulls in all the files specified by the #include statements. In this process, .i files are output. Often, the user wishes to examine the expanded program files in order to resolve conflicts or problems related to macroprocessing.

The second option, the -c option, suppresses the loading phase of the program. Only .o files are created. One might use this option to compile a module for syntax-checking purposes or to prepare modules for later linking with other modules. The .o files created can be linked with these other files on the command line.

For example, suppose you are creating a program called hangman.c, which uses some utility procedures you are creating in a file called util.c. After preparing the util.c file, you can compile it to check syntax like so:

```
$ cc -c util.c
```

Later, you can compile the hangman.c program and link it with the already-compiled util.o in the following way:

```
$ cc hangman.c util.o
```

The executable file created is still called **a.out**.

The third option, -o, allows you to specify an executable name other than the nondescript a.out. For example, in the previous example you might want the executable file to be called hangman. This can be accomplished in the following way:

```
$ cc -o hangman hangman.c util.o
```

The fourth option, -S, stops the processing before the assembler. Thus, assembly language, or .s, files are produced. These can be inspected for performance considerations, optimized, or used later. For example:

```
$ cc -S hangman.c
```

produces an assembly language program called hangman.s.

The next two options, -O and -g, are used for code optimization and to produce a symbol table for debugging purposes. We won't discuss the former at all; the latter subject is discussed later.

The last two options to be discussed are -I and -l. Both options take a pathname argument. -I allows you to specify the pathnames of directories containing include files and is useful if several persons are working on a project that uses the same include files. -l allows you to specify libraries that must be linked in with the object code. This option must be the last given in any sequence of more than one directive. Incidentally if you did want to compile a file, say `space.c`, with two options, say `-c` and `-O`, you would do it as follows:

```
$ cc -c -O space.c
```

4.3   Handling Errors

It is beyond the scope of this text to discuss the many program warnings and errors that the user can encounter in the course of compiling and linking C programs. A discussion of this is best left to your C language reference book.

However, one technique that can help is to redirect errors to a file. When a program with syntax errors is compiled, errors may be displayed to the screen too fast to read. These errors can be redirected to a file that can be looked at leisurely. This technique is called *redirecting standard error.*

Suppose you wish to compile `hangman.c` and direct the errors to a file called error. This is accomplished simply as:

```
$ cc hangman.c 2> error
```

The `2> error` part redirects the standard error to the file `error`. Of course this technique can be used in conjunction with any of the other compiler options or techniques we discussed previously in this chapter.

4.4   Some Debugging Tips

Your program can suffer from two kinds of errors—syntactic and logic.

Syntactic or *syntax* errors arise from the failure to satisfy the rules of the language. A good compiler will always detect syntax errors, although the way that it reports the error can often be misleading.

For example, a missing } may not be detected until many lines after it should have appeared. Some compilers only report "syntax error" rather than, for example, "missing }."

In *logic errors*, the code adheres to the rules of the language but the algorithm that is specified is somehow wrong. Logic errors are more difficult to diagnose because the compiler cannot detect them, but a few basic rules may help you find and eliminate logic errors.

1. Document your program carefully. Ideally, each non-trivial line of code should include a comment. In the course of commenting, you may detect or prevent logical errors.

2. Use **printf** statements to output intermediate results at checkpoints in the code. This may help you determine where the logic has gone wrong.

3. In case of an error, comment out portions of the code until the program compiles and runs. Add in the commented out code, one feature at a time, checking to see that the program still compiles and runs. When the program either does not compile or runs incorrectly, the last code you added is involved in the logic error.

Finding and eliminating logic errors is more art than science, and your proficiency will only develop with time and practice.

4.5 Extended Syntax and Semantic Checking

While it is impossible to provide automatic logic validation and the compiler can only check for syntactical correctness, Unix does provide two tools that are helpful in eliminating logical errors.

One of these is called **lint**. As its name implies, **lint** is a nit-picker that does checking beyond that of an ordinary compiler. For example, C compilers are often not very particular about certain inconsistencies such as parameter mismatches, declared variables that are not used, and type checking. **lint** is, however. Often, very difficult bugs can be prevented or diagnosed by using **lint**.

lint is run by typing

```
$ lint name.c
```

where `name.c` is a file or list of files to be formatted.

Another Unix tool, the C beautifier, or **cb** , is simply used to transform a sloppy-looking program into a readable one. **cb** does not change the program code. Instead it just adds plenty of tabs, line feeds, and spaces where needed to make things look nice. This is very helpful in finding badly matched or missing curly braces, erroneous if-then-else and case statements, and incorrectly terminated functions. As with **lint**, **cb** is run by typing **cb** and a file name at the command prompt; for example:

```
$ cb name.c
```

where name.c is a file or list of files to be checked. However, the output of
cb is to standard I/O so it needs to be redirected to a new file of a different
name. For example, to create a beautified file called **bname.c** from **name.c**,
type

```
$ cb name.c  > bname.c
```

Note that redirecting the output to the same file name will destroy the file!

4.6   Symbolic Debugging

sdb is a generic name for symbolic debugger—a debugger that lets you
single-step through C language code and view the results of each step. Various other debuggers are supported by different machines, including **dbx**
and **adb** but we will focus on **sdb** because it is a standard component of
Unix SVR4. While the complete set of **sdb** features is extensive, we can
learn enough simple commands to greatly increase our debugging capabilities.

When we wish to use the symbolic debugger, we first must compile the
sources involved with the **-g** option. This has the effect of including special
run-time code that interacts with the debugger. If the source code and
executable for program **sandwich** are in the current directory, we can run
sdb by typing

```
$ sdb sandwich
```

This will begin the **sdb** debugger. The program can be started normally
from the **sdb** debugger at any point by typing the **g** (for go) command
at the **sdb** prompt. However, we are more interested in single stepping
through the source code. Lines of code are displayed and executed one at
a time by using the **s** (for step) command. If the statement is a **printf**
or other output statement, it will output to the screen accordingly. If the
statement is a **scanf** or other input function, it will await your input. All
other statements execute normally.

At any point in the single-stepping process, individual variables can
be set or examined. For example, typing i!10 sets the variable i to 10.

Typing `i:?bd` displays the one byte contents of variable `i` in decimal. The permissible values for `l` and `m` and a summary of **sdb** commands are given in Table 4.4.

Command	Effect
g	Execute program continuously.
s	Single-step program.
S	Single-step over function call.

variable:?lm	Examine `variable` to `l` digits in format `m`.
	  l: b=byte, h=2 bytes, l=4 bytes
	  m: d=decimal, h=hex, o=octal, b=binary

t	Print stack trace.
T	Print the top line of the stack trace.
x	Print contents of the machine's registers.
w	Print a window of 10 lines around the current line.
z	Print the current line and next 9 lines and set the current line to last one printed.

Table 4.4: Some commonly used **sdb** commands

Very often when debugging a new program, the Unix system will abort execution and indicate that a *core dump* has occurred. This is a sure sign that your program has done something bad. A core dump creates a rather large file named `core`, which many programs simply remove before proceeding with the debugging. But `core` contains some valuable debugging information, especially when used in conjunction with **sdb**. For example, `core` contains the last line of the program that was executed and the contents of the function call stack at the time of the catastrophe. **sdb** can be used to single-step up to the point of the core dump to identify its cause. Later on, you may learn to use *breakpoints* to quickly come up to this line of code.

There are many other features of **sdb**, such as breakpoint setting, that the user should consult under **sdb(1)** in the Unix reference manual.

4.6.1 dbx and a Sample Session

We close this section with a sample session using a debugger that is found on many systems. The debugger **dbx** is in many ways similar to **sdb**, and the techniques used to identify errors are identical.

In this session we list the C program with **cat**. Then we compile and link it, and run the executable a.out. It is apparent that the program should stop if we enter anything but 1, but it does not stop. We next kill the program using <CTRL>-c and invoke **dbx**. Once in **dbx** we list the commands using the help feature. Notice their similarity to **sdb** commands. We then list some of the source code and decide to issue the **stop <var>** command. This will have the effect of setting a breakpoint that triggers whenever <var> is changed. We then start to execute the program with the **run** command. Execution stops as it reads the first input. We then issue a step command to continue executing one line at a time. On the very next executable line, execution is stopped because i has changed again. The debugger tells us that i was changed before the instruction on line 13 was executed, and gives the old and new values of i. This is obviously wrong, so we list the source code surrounding the line where i was changed and notice our mistake in the while loop—we used one equal sign instead of two.

```
$ cat test.c
#include <stdio.h>
#include <stdlib.h>

#define TRUE 1
#define FALSE 0

main()
{
int i=TRUE;

while(i = TRUE)
  {
     printf("\nEnter 1 to continue...");
     scanf("%d",&i);
  }

}

$cc -g test.c
$a.out

Enter 1 to continue...1

Enter 1 to continue...2
```

```
Enter 1 to continue...0

Enter 1 to continue...3

Enter 1 to continue...^C
$ dbx a.out
dbx version 2.10.2
Type 'help' for help.
(dbx) help
run                       - begin execution of the program
print <exp>               - print the value of the expression
where                     - print currently active procedures
stop at <line>            - suspend execution at the line
stop in <proc>            - suspend execution when <proc> is called
stop  <var>               - suspend execution if variable <var> change
cont                      - continue execution
step                      - single-step one line
next                      - step to next line (skip over calls)
trace <line#>             - trace execution of the line
trace <proc>              - trace calls to the procedure
trace <var>               - trace changes to the variable
trace <exp> at <line#>    - print <exp> when <line> is reached
status                    - print trace/stop's in effect
delete <number>           - remove trace or stop of given number
screen                    - switch dbx to another virtual terminal
call <proc>               - call a procedure in program
whatis <name>             - print the declaration of the name
list <line>, <line>       - list source lines
registers                 - display register set
quit                      - exit dbx
```

```
reading symbolic information ...
main:    9  int i=TRUE;
(dbx) list 1,20
     1  #include <stdio.h>
     2  #include <stdlib.h>
     3
     4  #define TRUE 1
     5  #define FALSE 0
     6
     7  main()
     8  {
>    9  int i=TRUE;
    10
    11  while(i = TRUE)
    12    {
    13        printf("\nEnter 1 to continue...");
    14        scanf("%d",&i);
    15    }
    16
    17  }
(dbx) stop i
[2] stop if changed i in main
(dbx) run

Enter 1 to continue...0
[2] i changed before [main: line 15]:
               new value = 0;
(dbx) step
[2] i changed before [main: line 13]:
               old value = 0;
               new value = 1;
  [main:13 ,0x4001c8]   printf("\nEnter 1 to continue...");
(dbx) list 10,13
    10
    11  while(i = TRUE)
    12    {
>*  13        printf("\nEnter 1 to continue...");
(dbx) quit
$
```

4.7 Performance Analysis and Tuning

As you hone your programming skills, you will wish to write programs that are not only correct but optimal. This term has several meanings, but in this case we mean that the execution speed of the program is as fast as possible. The Unix system provides two performance-tuning programs, **prof** and **gprof**, that can help you optimize the execution speed of your code.

Both of these programs help you identify what percentage of the processing time is being spent in a particular procedure so that you can concentrate your optimization efforts where they will do the most good—on the procedures that are taking the most time.

The **prof** program provides a *flat execution profile* for an executable program—the amount of time required by and the number of calls to a particular procedure. From this information you can identify which procedures are the most frequently used and which take the most time.

To use the **prof** program, you must specify the -p argument on the **cc** command line. After compiling the program, run it as usual. This creates a file called `mon.out` that is needed by **prof**. The **prof** program is then run on the executable file.

For example, if you wish to run the profiler on a source program consisting of a series of functions and procedures contained in file `sandwich.c`, you might do the following

```
$ cc -p -o sandwich sandwich.c
$ sandwich
$ prof sandwich
```

After **prof** is executed, the run-time statistics will be displayed as follows:

%time	cumsecs	#call	ms/call	name
1.0%	8.42	2.00	4.21	__doprnt
0.5%	4.33	1.00	4.33	__doscan
0.6%	5.12	1.00	5.12	__wrtchk
1.3%	10.30	2.00	5.15	__xflsbuf
0.6%	5.17	1.00	5.17	_exit
1.4%	11.60	2.00	5.80	_ioctl
1.4%	11.60	2.00	5.80	_isatty
1.5%	12.20	2.00	6.10	_localeconv
0.8%	6.70	1.00	6.70	_main
3.2%	25.50	3.00	8.50	_malloc
2.2%	18.00	2.00	9.00	_memchr
1.1%	9.05	1.00	9.05	_on_exit
1.2%	10.00	1.00	10.00	_open
3.0%	24.40	2.00	12.20	_printf
1.5%	12.40	1.00	12.40	_profil
1.7%	13.50	1.00	13.50	_read
9.0%	72.33	3.00	24.11	_sandwich
6.2%	50.20	2.00	25.10	_bread
3.3%	26.25	1.00	26.25	_cheese
23.6%	189.70	7.00	27.10	_ham
3.9%	31.10	1.00	31.10	_mustard
3.9%	31.15	1.00	31.15	_scanf
5.0%	40.12	1.00	40.12	_strcpy
10.2%	82.20	2.00	41.10	_write

The name column lists the procedure or function name (with an underscore prepended). You may note from the example that many of the procedures displayed are library routines that are linked invisibly by **cc**. The #call column lists the number of times that procedure or function was called, while the ms/call column lists the time needed to execute that procedure or function once. Finally, the cumsecs column is calculated as the product of the #call and ms/call columns, and the %time column lists the percentage of time spent in that procedure or function.

In this example, since 23% of the processing time is spent in procedure ham, it is a likely candidate for optimization.

The second profiling tool, **gprof**, is similar to **prof** except that in addition to the execution statistics, a function call graph is also generated. The function call graph represents function names as nodes and function calls as edges. The cumulative execution time for each sub-tree is listed on the graph. This feature helps to identify the execution times for groups of functions.

gprof is run by compiling the source code with the -gp option (or -pg on some compilers), then executing the program and running **gprof** on the executable and the graph monitor output generated by the compiler, gmon.out. For example, if in the previous example we wished to run **gprof** instead of **prof**, we would have typed:

```
$ cc -gp -o sandwich sandwich.c
$ sandwich
$ gprof sandwich gmon.out
```

4.8   Code and Program Maintenance

The Unix operating system is fitted with several tools that encourage, in fact require, strict version control over source code. This kind of access restriction is quite important when handling programs consisting of a large number of files or when more than one individual is working on the same project. For example, it would be disastrous if two programmers decided to modify the same source code file simultaneously—one set of changes would be lost. Similarly, suppose that a project consists of dozens of source files along with header and include files. If a header file is changed, every single source file using that header file must be recompiled or very difficult-to-find bugs will be introduced. Thus, we will identify those special programs that Unix provides to avoid these kinds of situations.

4.8.1   sccs

Source code control system, or **sccs**, is a software project-management tool. It places strict control over the access of files related to a software project to prevent nasty things like two people editing the same file at the same time. In addition, **sccs** keeps track of issues such as who modified a file and when (and what changes were made), who can read certain files, and who can write certain files. This kind of control is crucial when developing large programs for which many people will have access. Most important, **sccs** provides a historical trail of all program changes, which can be immensely useful when tracking down bugs.

Since **sccs** is best used when more than one programmer is involved in a project, it is beyond the scope of the text to discuss it here. We can, however, briefly mention the four most important commands in the **sccs** command set. These are **admin**, **delta**, **get**, and **prs**. **admin** is used to create and administer projects in the source control system, **delta** is used to effect changes to sources in a project, **get** is used to officially extract a source from a project to make changes, and **prs** is used to print information about changes made to sources and their status.

For more information on **sccs**, the reader is referred his or her system user's manual.

4.8.2   make

The Unix **make** utility is designed to help manage the construction and maintenance of programs composed of many source, object, and include files.

While there are many intricacies in the use of **make** files, we provide only the necessary information to manage simple programs. **make** files are best illustrated by example. Suppose our program, sandwich, consisted of the following source files: `sandwich.c`, `bread.c`, `ham.c`, `cheese.c`, and `mustard.c`.

When we construct the executable file, `sandwich`, we normally have to compile those source files that have been modified and link all the sources. Rather than keep track of which files have been modified, **make** does this for us. Suppose we construct a file called `Makefile` that contains the following:

```
FILES=  sandwich.c bread.c ham.c cheese.c mustard.c
OBJECTS=sandwich.o bread.o ham.o cheese.o mustard.o

sandwich: ${OBJECTS}
          ld -o sandwich ${OBJECTS} -lc
```

The first line assigns the symbolic variable `FILES` to the list of source files while the second line assigns the symbolic variable `OBJECTS` to the list of objects.

The third line describes the fact that the program, `sandwich`, is dependent on the list of object files. In other words, these files must be up to date in order for `sandwich` to be up to date. If any source file changes, the corresponding object file must be remade by compiling. The last line in the file is the loader directive to create the executable file `sandwich`. (Note that one of the quirks of **make** is that it requires a `<TAB>` in front of **ld**).

If you had created the source files and then wished to compile and link them, you simply type `make sandwich`, and then you would see:

```
$ make sandwich

cc -c sandwich.c
cc -c bread.c
cc -c ham.c
cc -c cheese.c
cc -c mustard.c

ld -o sandwich sandwich.o bread.o ham.o cheese.o mustard.o -lc
```

The new executable would then be ready.

Suppose now that you decided to make a change only to the file `bread.c`. Then when you remade the executable file you would see the following:

```
$ make sandwich

cc -c bread.c

ld -o sandwich sandwich.o bread.o ham.o cheese.o mustard.o -lc
```

make detects that only one file has been changed, and recompiles that file only.

Any time you write and exit from the **vi** editor, the modify date and time is updated. But suppose you wished to recompile all source files. You are not sure if you edited them all and you don't want to go back into the editor and write each out to indicate that they need to be recompiled. Fortunately, a special Unix command, **touch**, allows you to indicate that one or more source files need to be recompiled. **touch** updates a files date of modification so that it appears as if it has been edited. For example, typing

```
$ touch *.c
```

will guarantee that **make** will recompile all source files whether they have been changed or not.

The reader is encouraged to look in his or her systems reference manual or the references given in the bibliography to discover how to take full advantage of the make utility.

4.8.3   Libraries and Archives

Often we create functions for one program that we may want to use later in other programs. For example, we may have created a series of functions to convert decimal numbers to Roman numerals, then convert them back and perform arithmetic using these numbers. If we use one of these functions, we will probably use the others; therefore, it makes sense to save them in a common file. To keep things straight, normally we save object code in one place and the source in another. A collection of the object code of related functions is called a *library*. An example of a library that you already use is the C standard language library.

Unix allows you to construct libraries using its archive program. An *archive* is simply a collection of files stored in some compressed format. The Unix archive program, **ar**, has the general command format:

ar *key [position] archive-name file1 file2 ... filen*

The key value controls whether **ar** is to add, update, extract, or list the contents of the archive. The key functions are summarized in Table 4.5.

Key	Action
d	Delete the named files from the archive.
q	Append files to archive without checking if files exist.
	Use to create an archive.
r	Put files into the new or existing archive. Replace if files exist.
	Use to update an existing archive.
ru	Same as r, except only replaces updated files.
	Use to update an existing archive.
ri	Same as r but requires a [position] argument.
	This is the file name to insert files before.
ra	Same as r but requires a [position] argument.
	This is the file name to insert files after.
v	Give file-by-file description of archive constituents.
x	Extract the named files from the archive.

Table 4.5: Archive program, **ar**, key values

For example, suppose that our Roman numeral functions are stored in source files `romtodec.c`, `dectorom.c`, and `romarith.c`, with corresponding object files `romtodec.o`, `dectorom.o`, and `romarith.o`, respectively. We wish to create an archive called `roman.a` containing these files. It is traditional to name archives with an `.a` extension. In addition, **ld** will look for named files with such an extension. To create our archive we would use

```
ar q roman.a romtodec.o dectorom.o romarith.o
```

To view the contents of this archive, type:

```
ar t roman.a
```

The **ar** program can also create archives of source files; for example, if we wanted to put the source files in an archive called `romansource.a`, we would type

```
ar q romansource.a romtodec.c dectorom.c romarith.c
```

Note 4.1 *On Berkeley Unix, the command* **ranlib** *converts an archive file to a form that can be searched more rapidly.*

4.9   Exercises

1. Define the following terms:

    (a) compiler

    (b) assembler

    (c) assembly language

    (d) optimization

    (e) object code

    (f) machine language

    (g) linker

    (h) linking loader

2. What are the functions and program names associated with the phases of compilation performed by the **cc** command?

3. What command statement would be needed to invoke **cpp**, **ccom**, and **as** for program `test.c`?

4. What command statement would be needed to invoke **ld** program `test.o`?

5. What command statement is needed to invoke **cpp**, **ccom**, and **c2** for program foobar.c?

6. Write out the command to compile a program called `darts.c`.

7. Write out the command to compile a program called `maze.c` and output an executable file called **maze**.

8. Write out the command to compile two programs called `apple.c` and `pear.c` and link it to an object file called `banana.o`. The output should be an executable file called **banana**.

9. Write out the command to compile a program called `goldrush.c`, with optimization, and output it to an executable file, called **game**.

10. Write out the command to compile a program called `goldrush.c`, with optimization, output it to an executable called **game**, and output all compiler diagnostics to a file called **error**.

11. What other compiler options are available for your compiler and what do they do?

12. Why do you think that it is impossible to bypass the preprocessor phase of the compilation process?

13. Run the **lint** nit-picker on every C program available in your directory. What kinds of warnings do you get?

14. Run the C-beautifier program, **cb** , on any C program in your directory. Use the **diff** command to see what changes have been made.

15. Compile and run a C program using the -p option and the profiler program. Alter the program so that it is more or less efficient. Recompile and run the profiler again, noting any differences.

16. Compile and run a C program using the -gp option and the graph profiler program. Alter the program so that it is more or less efficient. Recompile and run the profiler again, noting any differences.

17. Suppose we wished to add the object file `romanout.o` to our `roman.a` archive. What is the archiver command line needed if we wish to insert the file before `dectorom.o`?

18. What is the archiver command line needed to extract `romtodec.c` from the source archive `romansource.a`?

19. Construct a makefile for the program `roman` that depends on source files, `roman.c`, `romtodec.c`, `dectorom.c`, and `romarith.c`.

20. Experiment with the symbolic debugger, **sdb**.

Appendix A

The Login Profile .profile

Each time a user logs in to a Unix system, two shell scripts are executed to initialize the user's environment: `/etc/profile`, the system profile, and `.profile`, the user's login profile contained in his or her home directory. The system administrator maintains the system profile. However, each individual user maintains his or her own login profile. The administrator provides each user with a default login profile when his or her account is created. After that, it's all up to the user.

The file `.profile` is a shell script—an ASCII file that contains a series of shell commands, shell programming constructs, and comments. A user can modify his or her login profile and, thus, his or her initial environment, using a text editor such as **vi**. A user edits his or her login profile by adding, modifying, or removing commands as needed. Once modifications are complete, the user either logs off and on again or executes `.profile` using the following syntax:

```
$ . .profile<CR>
$ _
```

This syntax causes the shell to update its own environment by executing the program without invoking a child process.

Prior to modifying their `.profile`, most users make a copy of it. This protects the file against accidental destruction and allows the user to restore it in case modifications don't work out as desired.

Login profiles vary greatly from user to user so a comprehensive treatment is not practical. However, there are a few essential elements common to many login profiles that are covered in this appendix.

A.1   The `PATH` Variable

The `PATH` variable contains a list of pathnames that refer to directories that the shell searches for command programs. Most users add additional pathnames to the default `PATH` value so that additional commands can be invoked by name alone, that is, without using a full pathname. Commands are located in various directories, as the following explains. Some of the common locations for user commands are:

- `/bin` traditionally contains essential user commands. However, with SVR4, `/bin` is soft-linked to `/usr/bin`.

- `/usr/bin` is another traditional location for user commands.

- `/usr/sbin` contains the System V version of many user commands.

- `/usr/5bin` is another location of System V commands.

- `/usr/ucb` contains the BSD version of many user commands.

- `/usr/lbin` is commonly used for *local commands*, that is, for commands that are specific to the local Unix installation.

- `/usr/local/bin` is another location for local commands.

- `/usr/add-on/bin` is a common location for user commands related to add-on software packages.

These directories may or may not be present, depending on the installation. See the system administrator for additional information.

To demonstrate setting the PATH variable, suppose that the default PATH value is `/usr/bin`. To add the pathnames of the directories containing BSD, System V, and local commands to the PATH variable, include the following commands in `.profile`:

```
PATH=$PATH:/usr/sbin:/usr/ucb:/usr/lbin
export PATH
```

This example emphasizes System V commands over BSD since `/usr/sbin` appears prior to `/usr/ucb`. To emphasize BSD commands, substitute the following PATH assignment:

```
PATH=$PATH:/usr/ucb:/usr/sbin:/usr/lbin
```

Finally, stronger emphasis can be placed on BSD commands with the following PATH assignment:

```
PATH=/usr/ucb:$PATH:/usr/sbin:/usr/lbin
```

This PATH value insures that the BSD version of any command is executed instead of a System V or local version. Equivalent emphasis on System V calls for the following PATH assignment:

```
PATH=/usr/sbin:$PATH:/usr/ucb:/usr/lbin
```

A.2   The TERM Variable

The TERM variable specifies a user's terminal type. For instance, to specify a vt100 terminal type, include the following commands in `.profile`:

```
TERM=vt100
export TERM
```

Other terminal types are specified in the same manner using the appropriate value in place of vt100.

A.3   Terminal Settings

The login profile is commonly used to define various terminal driver control
characters and settings with the **stty** command. Most users assign the
backspace character (CTRL-h) as the erase character and set the terminal
driver so that erase characters are echoed. To make these two assignments,
include the following commands in .profile:

```
stty erase '^h'
stty echoe
```

A.4   A Sample Login Profile

A login profile incorporating all of these examples would contain the following lines. Pound-sign characters (#) precede comments.

```
#
# Add the System V, BSD, and local bin directories
# to the PATH.
#
PATH=$PATH:/usr/sbin:/usr/ucb:/usr/lbin

#
# Set the terminal type to vt100.
#
TERM=vt100

#
# Export the PATH and TERM variables to the environment.
#
export PATH TERM

#
#  Set the erase character to a backspace.
#
stty erase '^h"

#
# Echo erase characters to the screen.
#
stty echoe
```

Appendix B

The User's Reference Manual

A complete set of Unix documentation consists of several extensive volumes, many of which are of interest primarily to the system administrator. However, all users should be familiar with and comfortable using the User's Reference Manual. In addition, programmers should be familiar with the Programmer's Reference Manual.

In some cases, both the User's and Programmer's Reference manuals are presented in a single volume. However, it is common for these documents to be contained in separate volumes. Unix manuals may be provided by the Unix vendor or the local installation, or they may be purchased commercially by the individual user. In some cases, vendors of PC Unix packages provide only installation manuals, forcing the user to rely commercially available references.

Reference manuals should be self-explanatory. However, Unix manuals are somewhat notorious for being terse, dense, at times confusing, and not at all self-explanatory despite their authors' best intentions. Therefore, this appendix contains a few pointers to aid our readers in getting started with Unix reference material—in particular, the User's and Programmer's Reference manuals.

B.1   Manual Sections

Unix reference material is traditionally divided into sections. Each section consists of an alphabetically presented series of related topics. For example, user commands are usually described in Section 1. Each topic is presented in a self-contained unit called a *manual page* or *man page*. The term *manual page* should not be taken literally since any one topic may occupy several printed pages. Instead, it refers to a format or set of conventions used to describe commands, subroutines, and other Unix related topics. Each manual page contains sections and subsections that cover a variety of subjects applicable to the manual page's topic. The format of manual pages is generally consistent within a manual section but varies from section to section. However, the format and content of an individual manual page may be tailored to the topic so that the topic is described thoroughly.

Section 1 describes user commands. Section 2 covers C language system calls, that is, it describes the programmer's interface to the Unix kernel's services. Section 3 discusses C language subroutines. Subroutines differ from system calls in that they provide additional benefit to the programmer above and beyond the primitive utility of system calls. In many cases, subroutines are founded on specific system calls, for example, file system calls, but provide a useful layer of abstraction above the system call level. In other cases, subroutines are general programming routines, such as string handling and mathematical routines, that are unrelated to specific kernel services. Finally, certain subroutines provide optimum performance and higher reliability than might be achieved by direct use of system calls. Section 4 describes the specific format of files that are commonly used among several commands, system calls, or subroutines. This section typically includes the C language structure definition and refers to the appropriate header file. Section 5 contains miscellaneous information of interest to Unix users and programmers.

The manual pages in Section 1 of the User's Reference Manual contains general user commands. Certain commands, such as system administration commands, are omitted from this manual. In Section 1 of the Programmer's Reference Manual, manual pages show programmer related commands, such as **cc**, and Sections 2, 3, 4, and 5. Each section includes a *table of contents*, a *permuted index*, and an *intro page*. The table of contents lists the topics covered in the manual section. The permuted index is a permutation of the table of contents. It presents, in three separate columns, an alphabetical list of key topics from the table of contents, the associated section entry, and the portion of the table of contents entry that doesn't appear in the key topic column. Key topics appear in the center column. The appropriate manual page is identified to its right, and the remainder from the table of contents appears to its left. The intro page is the first manual page in each section. It describes the section briefly and presents any essential information that is not contained in the manual pages themselves.

B.2   Section 1 — User Commands

Section 1 describes user commands. Manual pages in Section 1 are organized as follows:

- **NAME** gives the name of the command and a summary of its purpose. Section 1 manual pages are alphabetized according to **NAME**. Occasionally, several related commands are presented in a single manual page. For example, **sh**, **jsh**, the job control shell, and **rsh**, the restricted shell, are described together. In such cases, **NAME** lists each command covered in the manual page.

- **SYNOPSIS** presents the complete syntax for the command or commands.

- **DESCRIPTION** contains a description of what the command does and how it is used. This section covers all command options and arguments.

- **EXAMPLES** gives examples of the command's use.

- **DIAGNOSTICS** explains error messages and return values.

- **FILES** lists any files related to the command or commands.

- **SEE ALSO** lists related commands and topics that are covered in separate manual pages as well as additional sources of information.

- **NOTES** contains additional information regarding the command or commands.

- **BUGS** lists any known bugs.

NAME, **SYNOPSIS**, and **DESCRIPTION** are mandatory. The remaining sections appear as needed.

B.3   Sections 2 and 3 — System Calls and Subroutines

Section 2 describes C language system calls. Section 3 describes C language subroutines. In some manuals, Section 3 is subdivided as follows:

- **3C** contains C language library routines.

- **3E** contains executable and linking format library routines.

- **3G** contains general purpose library routines.

- **3M** contains the math library routines.

- **3S** contains the standard input/output library routines.

- **3X** contains specialized library routines.

Manual pages in Sections 2 and 3 are organized as follows:

- **NAME** gives the name of the function call and a summary of its purpose. Section 2 and 3 manual pages are alphabetized by **NAME**. Several related functions may be described in a single manual page. In such cases, all of the related functions are listed under **NAME**.

- **SYNOPSIS** lists any required header files and the complete syntax for each function call. Include statements depict required header files. With the release of SVR4, system call and subroutine syntax is depicted with ASNI C function prototypes. Older manuals may use the original K&R syntax.

- `DESCRIPTION` describes the purpose of the system call, its behavior, and how to use it.

- `EXAMPLES` contains code fragments depicting a typical use of the system call.

- `SEE ALSO` identifies related user commands, system calls, and additional sources of information.

- `NOTES` contains additional information pertaining to the system call.

- `DIAGNOSTICS` describes return and error codes.

`NAME`, `SYNOPSIS`, and `DESCRIPTION` are mandatory. The remaining sections appear as needed.

For Section 3 subroutines, libraries that are needed during the link phase are identified either in the manual page or the Section 3 intro page.

Appendix C

vi Command Summary

Command	Effect
h	Move cursor left one character
l	Move cursor right one character
k	Move cursor up one line
j	Move cursor down one line
w	Move cursor to start of next word
b	Move cursor to first character of current or previous word
e	Move cursor to last character of current or next word
^	Move cursor to first non-whitespace character of current line
0	Move cursor to first character of current line including whitespace
$	Move cursor to last character of current line
−	Move cursor to first non-whitespace character of previous line
+	Move cursor to first non-whitespace character of next line
<CR>	Move cursor to first non-whitespace character of next line
H	Move cursor to first non-whitespace character of line at top of window
M	Move cursor to first non-whitespace character of line at center of window
L	Move cursor to first non-whitespace character of line at bottom of window
(	Move cursor to start of next sentence
)	Move cursor to end of current sentence
{	Move cursor to start of next paragraph
}	Move cursor to end of current paragraph
nG	Move cursor/window to line n of the file
G	Move cursor/window to the last line of the file
<CTRL-d>	Scroll window forward a half screen
<CTRL-u>	Scroll window backward a half screen
<CTRL-f>	Scroll window forward a full screen
<CTRL-b>	Scroll window backward a full screen

Table C.1: Cursor-movement commands

Command	Effect
a*text*<ESC>	Append *text* after cursor
A*text*<ESC>	Append *text* at end of line
i*text*<ESC>	Insert *text* before cursor
I*text*<ESC>	Insert *text* before first non-whitespace character
o*text*<ESC>	Open new line after current line and insert *text*
O*text*<ESC>	Open new line before current line and insert *text*

Table C.2: Append and insert commands

Command	Effect
cnw$text$<ESC>	Change n words to $text$
C$text$<ESC>	Change through the end of line to $text$
$n$cc$text$<ESC>	Change n lines to $text$
rα	Replace current character with α
R$text$<ESC>	Replace typed-over characters with $text$
s$text$	Substitute $text$ for character at cursor position
S$text$	Substitute $text$ for current line

Table C.3: Change, replace, and substitute commands

Command	Effect
nx	Delete n characters
nd<SPACE>	Delete n characters
$n$dw	Delete n words
$n$dd	Delete n lines
D	Delete to end of line
nd)	Delete n sentences
nd}	Delete n paragraphs

Table C.4: Text deletion commands

Command	Effect
p	Put text from temporary register after the cursor
np	Put n copies of temporary register after the cursor
P	Put text from temporary register before the cursor
yw	Yank current word into the temporary register
yy	Yank current line into the temporary register
Y	Same as yy
y$	Yank from cursor to end of line into the temporary register
y)	Yank sentence into the temporary register
y}	Yank paragraph into the temporary register
nyα	Yank n copies of α into the temporary register

Table C.5: Move and copy commands

Command	Effect
"αp	Put from named buffer α
"αdβ	Delete object β and place in named buffer α
"αyβ	Yank object β and place in named buffer α

Table C.6: Using named registers

Command	Effect
w<CR>	Write buffer to file
w *newfile*<CR>	Write buffer to *newfile*
wq<CR>	Write buffer to file and exit
ZZ	Same as :wq
x,yw *file*	Write lines n through y to *file*
q<CR>	Quit – exit if no changes made
q!<CR>	Quit – exit and abandon any changes made

Table C.7: Write and quit commands

Command	Effect
fα	Move cursor right to character α
Fα	Move cursor left to character α
tα	Move cursor right and position it prior to character α
Tα	Move cursor left and position it after to character α
;	Repeat previous f or F command
/*text*/	Search forward for the first occurrence of *text*
?*text*?	Search backward for the first occurrence of *text*
n	Repeat previous / or ? command
N	Repeat previous / or ? command in reverse direction
//	Repeat previous / or ? command
??	Repeat previous / or ? command in reverse direction

Table C.8: Search commands

Command	Effect
m,n	Search lines m through n
$m,+n$	Search lines m through current line $+n$
$-m,$	Search current line $-m$ through current line
$.,+m$	Search current line to current line $+m$
$.,\$$	Search current line to end of file
$1,\$$	Search first line of file to end of file
%	Search entire file

Table C.9: Range specifications for the find and substitute command

Command	Effect
\>	End of word indicator
\<	Start of word indicator
[ ]	Character class definition
^	Match beginning of line
$	Match end of line
.	Match any single character
*	Match 0 or more occurrences of preceding character
[^]	Match any character except those listed
$l-u$	Lexical range l to u within character class

Table C.10: Meta-characters used in regular expressions

Command	Effect
u	Undo the last command
U	Return current line to its previous state

Table C.11: Undo commands

Command	Effect
.	Repeat last command
J	Join the current and next line together
<CTRL-v>	Print out non-printing character
<CTRL-1>	Clear and redraw screen
~	Change upper case to lower case and *vice versa*
:	Enter command line mode

Table C.12: Miscellaneous commands

Appendix D

Unix Commands Summary

This appendix contains a brief synopsis of the Unix commands and options discussed in the text.

admin install (source code) a file into the source code control system

ar key [position] archive name file1 [file2...] create or update an archive library file

as assemble an *assembler* language source code file producing an object code file

awk pattern matching and field processing text filter

cal [[month] year] print a calendar to standard output

cat [-s] [file ...] concatenate and print a file to standard output

cb file C language beautifier filter

cc [-cgIOPS] [-o name] [-llibname] C language compiler

cd [directory] change directory

chmod mode file1 [file2 ...] change a file's access mode

cpp C language pre-processor

cp [-ir] srcfile1 [srcfile2 ...] destfile copy files

csh C shell

delta install modifications to a (source code) file into source code control

diff list the differences between two text files

echo arg1 [arg2 ...] print arguments to standard output

env list the content of the shell's environment

exit exit from shell

export variable1 [variable2 ...] install variables into the shell's environment

file file1 [file2 ...] print a file's type

`find pathlist criteria action` find files in *pathlist* that satisfy *criteria* and execute *action*

`get` extract a (source code) file from the source code control system

`gprof file proffile` print an execution profile including a call graph

`grep [-l] regexpr [filename...]  search file(s) for regexpr`
\item \verbkill [-n] pid+ send a signal to a process

`ksh` Korn shell

`ld` link edit an object code file and produce an executable file

`lint` check a C source code file for syntax errors, bugs, and other unwanted fluff

`ln [ -s ] target newlink` link files, that is, create links

`lp [ -m ] [ -d prname ] file1 [ file2 ... ]` print a file on the system's printer

`ls [ -adlpxFC ] [ pathname... ]` list the content of a directory or information about a file

`mail [ userid... ]` send or read electronic mail

`make target` build an executable file

`mkdir [ -p ] newdir` create a new directory

`mv [ -i ] srcfile1 [ srcfile2 ... ] destfile` move a file

`nohup command` execute a command protected from hangup signal

`passwd` update a user's password

`pg [ -n ] [ file ... ]` print a file to standard output in pages

`prof file` print an execution profile

`prs` print statistics regarding a file under source code control

`pr [ -df ] [ -cols ] [ page ] [ -wW ] [ -lL ] [ -h header ] [ file ... ]+` format and print a file to standard output

`ps [ -u userid1 [ userid2 ... ] ] [ -f ]` print a process status report

pwd print pathname of current directory

rmdir directory1 [directory2 ...] remove a directory

rm [-i] file1 [file2 ...] remove a file

rm [-ri] dirname1 [dirname2 ...] [file ...] remove a directory and its content

rsh restricted Bourne shell

sccsdiff print differences between two files under source code control

sdb symbolic debugger

set print shell variables

sh Bourne shell

sort [-nu] [-tc] [m.n [-m.n]] [file ... **]**+ sort a text file

stty [-a] print terminal driver control character and parameter assignments

stty control-character value set terminal driver control character

stty option set terminal driver option

tail [-|n] [-bcf **] [** pathname ... **]**+ print tail of file to standard output

touch set a file's date of last modification

type cmd1 [cmd2 ...] print type of an executable file

umask [mode] print or modify the umask value

unget return a file to source code control without installing modifications

vi [[n]**]**+ visual editor

wc [-clw] [file ...] print a count of characters/lines/words in file

what print the version of an executable file

which print the path name of an executable file

who [**am i**] print a list of users logged on to the system or information about the user

Appendix E

Overview of Korn and C Shells

The Korn and C shells, **ksh** and **csh** respectively, offer a number of additional features over and above those of the Bourne shell. Both of these shells are released with SVR4. This appendix contains a brief overview of some of the additional features offered by the Korn and C shells. For a detailed presentation, the reader is referred to any of the several texts devoted exclusively to these topics.

E.1   Korn Shell – ksh

The Korn shell offers the user the following features beyond the capabilities of the Bourne shell:

- Additional programming constructs. These constructs include additional flow of control mechanisms and direct support for menus and menu selections.

- Command aliases. A user can define abbreviations for commonly used commands and override the `PATH` value by translating command names to full pathnames.

- Tilde substitution. **ksh** replaces a string of the form ˜*userid*, where *userid* is a valid login name for one of the system's users, with the full path of *userid*'s home directory.

- Alternate command substitution syntax. **ksh** treats a string of the form `$(`*command*`)`, where *command* is a Unix command, the same as `'`*command*`'`.

- Expanded support for shell and environment variables.

- Expanded support for file name generation. In particular, **ksh** allows file name matching using a list of patterns in place of a simple pattern.

- Job control. **ksh** includes mechanisms that provide additional control of and support for background processes.

- Commands history. **ksh** maintains a list of the most recent user commands and provides the user with access to that list via file search commands similar to those used in text editors. Futhermore, the user can select the editor to emulate, that is, can select the set of file search commands used by the shell to access the commands history.

- Command editing. **ksh** allows users to edit a command as it is typed or after it is selected from the commands history.

- Additional internal commands.

E.2   C Shell – csh

The C shell offers the following additional capabilities:

- additional programming constructs. The C shell is so named because its programming features are very similar to those of the C programming language.

- file name completion. A user can refer to files by typing partial file names that are completed by the shell itself. This differs from file name generation, which is also supported, in that the user does not type a pattern in addition to the partial file name.

- commands history. **csh** includes a commands history similar to that of **ksh**. However, the commands and functions used to access the commands history are defined by the shell and not based on emulation of a text editor.

- command aliases. This capability is similar to that of the Korn shell.

- job control of background processes.

- additional internal commands.

- expanded support for environment and shell variables.

Appendix F

Glossary

A

absolute path see **full path**.

access mode a file's complete set of access permissions.

archive generally, a collection of objects, such as text files, stored as a unit; in a Unix environment, often called an **archive library** or simply a **library**, a collection of executable functions (in object code format) stored in a single file suitable for linking into an executable program; often containing a group of related functions that provide a set of reusable programming utilities.

ANSI American National Standards Institute.

ANSI X3J11 ANSI standard definition for the C language.

ASCII American Standard Code for Information Interchange.

assembler a program that translates assembly language into machine code or object code.

assembly language a low-level programming language consisting primarily of symbolic representations of a processor's (CPU) instruction set.

B

background a means of executing a program such that the shell invokes a child process to carry out a user's command and then accepts the user's next command without waiting for its child process to complete; compare with **foreground**.

binary executable a program file whose instructions are in machine code form.

breakpoint a location or memory address where the execution of a program is suspended during debugging.

BSD Berkeley Software Distribution.

C

child directory a directory that descends from another directory, that is, a directory that is the successor of another directory; compare with **parent directory**.

command language script a program whose instructions are sequences of Unix commands and shell programming constructs; ASCII text files.

command line in the shell, a command typed by a user; in **vi**, the input area displayed while **vi** is in extended command mode.

command mode the mode in which **vi** interprets keys typed by the user as simple commands that perform operations such as entering edit mode, moving the cursor, and deleting text. Compare with **edit mode** and **extended command mode**.

command processor the Unix program that accepts and interprets user commands from the keyboard.

command programs Unix user commands that are separate, stand-alone programs; also called **external commands**.

command prompt a character or text string that indicates the shell is ready and waiting for the user's command.

compiler generally, a program or series of programs that translate high-order language source code files, such as C language source files, into an executable program. The Unix C compiler **cc** can also translate a C language source file into several different forms, including assembler language and object code.

control character generally, a character, such as <CTRL-d>, that is generated by simultaneously pressing the control key and some other key; with respect to the terminal driver, a character that is processed as an instruction to the driver itself.

core dump a file that contains the memory image of a process at the moment that it encountered an irrecoverable error; used in conjunction with a debugger such as **sdb** to determine the cause of the fatal error.

CPU Central Processing Unit.

cursor a symbol that indicates where the next key typed by the user will appear either on a command line or in the **vi** edit buffer.

D

data segment the portion of a binary executable file that contains static data elements encoded by the programmer; it may contain any type of data including ASCII strings, binary integers, binary floating point numbers, pointers.

DEC Digital Equipment Corporation.

device another term for the special file associated with a peripheral, such as a printer or terminal, or a reference to the peripheral itself.

directory a file used by the operating system to associate file names with files and to organize the file system.

directory hierarchy all directories that are accessible to a Unix system's users, that is, all directories that descend from a system's root directory.

distributed file system see **remote file system**.

dot a file name that refers to the directory which contains it.

dot-dot a file name that refers to the parent of the directory that contains it.

E

edit buffer a area of memory that holds the text for a file being edited under **vi**.

edit mode the mode in which **vi** inserts characters typed by the user into the edit buffer except for <ESC>, <CTRL-h>, and <CTRL-w>. Compare with **command mode** and **extended command mode**.

edit session the sequence of events that occurs after invoking and prior to exiting the editor.

edit window the range of lines displayed by **vi**.

environment a subset of the shell's variables that is passed to each process invoked by the shell.

erase character the terminal driver control character used to delete a character from the current line; the default is **#**.

escaping a character a technique that masks the special meaning of meta-characters and thus causes the shell to treat it as a literal; sometimes called **quoting** a character.

executable another term for a binary executable program file.

execute permission grants or denies the associated class of users the right to execute a program file or to use a directory in a path name.

extended command mode the mode in which **vi** reads and executes a complex user command such as searching for and replacing text. Compare with **edit mode** and **command mode**.

F

file name a sequence of characters that identifies a file, that is, the name portion of a directory entry (link).

file name generation a method of referring to files and directories using representative text patterns instead of literal file names.

file system the Unix means of storing, organizing, and accessing files as well as the interface to the computer's hardware devices.

filter a program that performs an operation, such as sorting, or a translation, such as replacing lowercase with uppercase, on its standard input and produces the result on its standard output.

flat execution profile with respect to an executable program, the amount of time required by and the number of calls to a particular procedure; this is provided by the utility **prof**.

foreground the default means of executing a program in which the shell invokes a child process to carry out a user's command and waits for its child to complete prior to accepting another command. Compare with **background**.

full path or absolute path a pathname that starts with a slash character (/), that is, a pathname that uses the root directory as its reference point; and refers to a distinct file regardless of the current directory. Compare with **relative path**.

G

group an association of users who have something in common; the user group associated with a file.

group ID an integer that uniquely identifies a user group.

209

H

hard link a directory entry that refers to a file via its inode; a hard link provides direct access to a file.

header with respect to a binary executable file, it describes the file so that the loader can properly transfer it to memory; with respect to C language source code, it contains function prototypes, data structure and symbol definitions, code macros.

home directory a directory, specified in the password file, that is a user's current directory during and immediately following the login sequence.

host computer on which the command processor is running, and on which the user is logged on.

I

inode a system table that contains a file's disk layout and other vital information.

internal command a Unix command that is an internal part of the shell. Compare with **command programs**.

interrupt signal a hardware signal generally used to initiate an asynchronous process or to handle an anomalous program condition.

I/O Input/Output.

I/O data streams a program's collection of input and output channels; conceptualized and handled as files.

I/O redirection a shell mechanism for redefining a process's I/O data streams, in particular standard input, output, and error; occurs on a process-by-process basis.

ISO/OSI International Standards Organization/Open Systems Interconnection reference model.

J

K

kernel the functional core of a Unix operating system.

kernel call a kernel service routine; kernel calls are used to create and manage processes, to access and manipulate the file system, and manage the system's resources.

kill character the terminal driver control character used to delete the current line; The default kill character is @.

L

library see **archive**.

line a sequence of ASCII words terminated by a newline character.

link a directory entry, that is, a reference to a file; see **hard link** and **soft link**.

link count the number of (hard) links that refer to a particular file.

linker a program that prepares relocatable object code for execution, thus producing a binary executable file.

linking loader a program that performs the functions of a linker and in addition loads the program into main memory for execution.

logic error an error in which a program or function compiles and executes but produces an undesired result; that is, a program or function whose behavior is flawed even though its source code adheres to the rules of the source language.

login name identifies an individual as an authorized user of a Unix system; often called a **login ID** or simply a **login**.

login prompt a text string, issued during the login sequence, that indicates the system is ready to accept a user's login name.

M

machine code binary program instructions that are executable directly by a system's CPU; often called **machine language** or **object code**.

mail electronic messages sent from one user to another.

meta-characters the special characters used in file name patterns and regular expressions.

MS-DOS Microsoft's Disk Operating System.

multiplier a positive integer used in **vi** to multiply the effect of some command.

N

named pipe a pipe that has at least one directory entry and is generally accessible.

newline character an invisible line terminator/separator.

news messages posted to all users by the system administrator.

node name a symbolic name or address by which a Unix system is known to other systems on a network.

null nothingness or a lack of value; a **null device** (`/dev/null`) accepts input but has no output and no function, a **null** shell variable has no value, a **null character** is an empty character; distinct from non-printing or blank characters, which have a definite value.

O

object code see **machine code**.

optimization a step in compilation that improves an aspect or characteristic of a program; programs can be optimized in terms of execution time, and memory usage, among other things.

ordinary file a randomly addressable sequence of bytes organized and stored on some permanent media such as a magnetic disk.

other the default user group consisting of all users who are not assigned to a specific group.

owner with respect to a file, the user who is authorized to change a file's access mode and ownership; in general, a file's owner is the user who created it.

P

parent directory a directory that has at least one descendant directory, that is, a directory that is the predecessor of at least one other directory. Compare with **child directory**.

password a text string, associated with a login ID, that confirms the identity of a user.

password aging a security precaution in which a Unix system periodically requires users to change their passwords.

password file a system administration file that contains, among other things, the login name, home directory, and default shell for each system user. Prior to SVR4, the password file also contained the encrypted passwords of the system's users. SVR4 provides an additional measure of protection by hiding the location of the file that contains the encrypted user passwords.

password prompt a text string issued during the login sequence that indicates the system is ready to accept a user's password.

PATH a system variable that contains a list of directories that are searched by the shell for executable programs.

pathname a file reference that consists of at least a file name optionally preceded by a list of directory names; directory names in the list are separated by slash characters (/). See also **full path** and **relative path**.

PC personal computer.

peripheral any input/output device or secondary storage.

permissions commands that grant or deny each of a file's three user classes (owner, group, and other) the right to read, write, or execute a file. See **read permission**, **write permission**, and **execute permission**.

PID see **process ID**.

pipe a one-way, first in/first out data channel between two or more processes.

pipeline in command line, a sequence of commands separated by pipe characters (|); in processes, an arrangement between two or more processes where the output of one is fed, as input, to a second; the output of the second is fed to a third, and so forth. A pipeline command line gives rise to a pipeline of processes.

predecessor see **parent directory**.

primary storage short-term storage consisting of the CPU's address space.

process an instance of a program executing under a Unix operating system.

process ID an integer which uniquely identifies a process.

program any file which is executable by the operating system.

PS1 the system prompt variable.

Q

quoting a character see **escaping a character**.

R

read permission grants or denies the associated class of users the right to read a file.

redirecting standard error a technique whereby the output from standard error is redirected to a file or device.

register in **vi**, a memory buffer used to store and retrieve text.

relative path a pathname that starts with something other than a slash character and uses the current directory as a reference point. A given relative path may refer to different files, depending on the current directory.

remote file system a file system accessible to one or more systems, other than its physical host, over a network; a file system residing on one host system that is attached to the root file system of a separate computer.

root directory the ancestor of all other directories in a Unix system.

root user see **super user**.

S

sane a **stty** option that instructs the terminal driver to adopt a rational set of control-characters and operational parameters; usually used when a user's terminal behaves erratically.

SCO Santa Cruz Operation.

secondary storage long-term storage devices such as disks and tapes.

shell a Unix command processor.

shell program see **shell script**.

shell script a program file consisting of a series of Unix commands and shell programming constructs. Shell scripts are ASCII text files.

shell variable a name-value pair created and maintained by the shell; often used to specify operational parameters to the shell.

soft link a directory entry that refers to a file via another directory entry and provides indirect access to a file. Compare with **hard link**.

special file a point of interface to one of the computer's hardware devices or a synchronized communications channel (pipe) between cooperating programs.

standard error the I/O stream, usually associated with the user's terminal display, where (by convention) a program outputs error messages and diagnostic information.

standard input the I/O stream, usually associated with the user's keyboard, where (by convention) a program reads its input.

standard output the I/O stream, usually associated with the user's terminal display, where (by convention) a program writes its output, possibly excluding error and diagnostic messages.

sub-directory see **child directory**.

successor see **child directory**.

super user a user who is granted omnipotent access rights to a Unix system; generally the system's administrator, who is treated as the owner of the entire system.

SVID System V Interface Definition.

SVR3 System V Release 3.

SVR4 System V Release 4.

symbolic link see **soft link**.

syntactic error see **syntax error**.

syntax error an error in which the source code for a program or function fails to adhere to the rules of the source language.

system administrator the person or persons responsible for the operation of a Unix system.

system call see **kernel call**.

T

temporary buffer the memory area used by **vi** to store text that is removed or changed by commands; used by the undo and repeat commands.

TERM the system variable that identifies the user's terminal type.

terminal device an asynchronous input/output port to which a user's terminal is connected.

terminal driver a systems program that manages asynchronous input/output ports, that is, terminal devices.

text segment the portion of a binary executable file that contains the machine language instructions.

trojan horse a method for penetrating a system's security measures that masquerades as a common command program, such as the **login** program, in order to collect information to invade a user's account or the system.

tty driver see **terminal driver**.

tty port see **terminal device**.

U

umask a value used to alter the default access mode of an ordinary file or directory that is subtracted from the default access mode to produce a new value for creating files and directories.

unix the filename of the Unix executable.

USL UNIX System Laboratories.

unnamed pipe a pipe that does not have a directory entry, that is, a pipe which is accessible only to its creator and users.

user account consists of a login name, a password, a home directory, and some administrative files.

user ID an integer that uniquely identifies a system user.

V

W

whitespace non-printing characters including the space and tab characters.

words with respect to **vi**, any sequence of alphanumeric characters terminated by whitespace, a punctuation mark, or other non-alphanumeric character; any string of adjacent punctuation marks or non-alphanumeric characters is also treated as a word.

write permission grants or denies the associated class of users the right to modify a file.

X

XENIX a Unix version produced and distributed explicitly for personal computers; originally developed by Microsoft and released in 1986 and currently distributed by Santa Cruz Operation (SCO) and Interactive Corporation.

Bibliography

[1] *The Bell System Technical Journal* 57, (July/August 1978).

[2] Ritchie, Dennis, M. "The Evolution of the UNIX Time-Sharing System," *Proceedings of the Symposium on Language Design and Programming Methodology* Sydney (September 1979):25-35.

[3] McGilton, Henry and Rachel Morgan, *Introducing the UNIX System* New York, McGraw-Hill, 1983.

[4] *The Bell System Technical Journal*, 63, (October 1984).

[5] *UNIX* System User's Manual: System V* Western Electric, Incorporated (1983).

[6] *UNIX System V User's Guide* AT&T (1984).

[7] Kernighan, Brian and Rob Pike, *The UNIX Programming Environment* Englewood Cliffs, N.J.: Prentice-Hall, Inc., 1984.

[8] Bach, Maurice, *The Design of the UNIX Operating System* Englewood Cliffs, NJ: Prentice-Hall, Inc., 1986.

[9] Bolsky, Morris I. and David G. Korn, *The KornShell Command and Programming Language*, Prentice Hall, Englewood Cliffs, NJ, 1989.

[10] Leffler, Samuel J. et al, *Implementation of the 4.3BSD UNIX Operating System*, Reading, Massachusetts: Addison Wesley, 1989.

[11] *UNIX SYSTEM V RELEASE 4 User's Reference Manual* Englewood Cliffs NJ,: Prentice-Hall, Inc., 1990.

[12] *UNIX SYSTEM V RELEASE 4 Programmer's Reference Manual*, Englewood Cliffs, NJ: Prentice-Hall, Inc., 1990.

[13] Stevens, W. Richard, *UNIX NETWORK PROGRAMMING*, Prentice-Hall, Inc., Englewood Cliffs, 1990.

[14] Kernighan, Brian W., and Dennis M. Ritchie, *The C Programming Language*, 2d ed., Englewood Cliffs, NJ: Prentice-Hall, Inc., 1990.

[15] "Capital C" *IEEE Spectrum* (February, 1992):13-14.

Appendix G

Index

yank and put commands, 134-
35
Thompson, Ken, 6
touch command, 171
Trojan horse, 36, 37
tty driver. *See* terminal driver
type command, 79
Typing errors, correcting, 42

Undo commands, in **vi**, 143, 191
UNIX System Laboratories
(USL), 6, 7
User account, 34
User ID, 22
User's Reference Manual, 182
Using named registers, in **vi**,
134-35, 190

---

vi command,
cursor movement, 114-20
command line arguments, 112-
13
defined, 108-10
editing features, 146-50
escape to shell, 148
exiting, 135-37
modes, 113-14
recovering edits, 149
searching for text, 137-43
starting, 111-12
summary 187-92
window movement, 120

---

wc command, 94
which command, 92
who command, 50
Word count command, 94
Word searching commands, in **vi**,
138
Write, with file access, 22
Write and quit commands, in **vi**,
135-37, 190

XENIX, 7, 8